BLESSED TO ANNOUNCE

From Walk-On to Team Captain
The Pathway to Success For Collegiate Athletes

Andrew Capirchio

ISBN: 978-0-578-45898-4

ACKNOWLEDGEMENTS

THIS BOOK WOULDN'T be possible without the endless love and support I have received from my family, friends, and teammates who were there every step of the way. The inspiration for this book came from the incredible stories and experiences I shared with these people during my athletic career.

I can count on my hands the number of sporting events my parents missed throughout my career. To my parents, Craig and Jeanine Capirchio, I am forever indebted for your continual sacrifices and long nights to provide the opportunities I've had along this journey. The valuable lessons, knowledge, and support you provided me are irreplaceable. The work ethic you instilled in me from a young age set the standard very high. The hundreds of home-cooked meals, hugs after games, and long phone calls always provided a sense of love and security no matter how far away you were. Thank you to my older brother, Carter, for your constant domination of me in every sport through our childhood. You exposed me to my first sense of competition and growth as an athlete during those losses. Thank you to my younger twin brothers, Sam and

Henry, for your continual love, support, and effortless supply of humor.

Thank you to my loved ones who aren't with us. Your spirit is never forgotten and your influence is undeniable. My grandfather, David Capirchio, who was my biggest fan. I would love to watch one more Diamondbacks game on the living room couch with you. My aunt, Janey McDonald, and her husband, my uncle, Paul McDonald, for showing our family the true meaning of grace in strength as they battled cancer for many years with nothing but a smile and big hearts. Thank you to all my extended family, you have always been my biggest fans, and I am grateful for the support from Devils Lake, North Dakota, as well as Northern California.

A special thank you to my other family who I spent seasons with on the gridiron from Fountain Hills Pop Warner, Scottsdale Pop Warner, Fountain Hills High School, Scottsdale Community College, and Concordia University-St. Paul. We are forever teammates and the memories we created will last a lifetime. There was always someone available to pick up the phone when I needed it. None of the stories or advice shared in this book would be possible without all of you.

Thank you to my academic teachers and professors who pushed me in the classroom. Dr. Steve Borick of Scottsdale Community College and Mr. Matthew Johnson of Fountain Hills High School. You challenged me in ways I had never imagined, changing my perspective as a student and person.

Thank you to my coaches who expected nothing less than my best and saw potential in me when others did not. Specifically, Coach Doug Madoski of Scottsdale Community College for allowing me the opportunity to walk on to his program. My experiences as a junior college athlete forever changed my life for the better. Thank you, Luke Salzman, Jim Fairfield, Airabin Justin, Ayrius Justin, Darrell Dawson, Tommy Ziegler, Luke Jaicks, Kate Engard, Brandon Moore, Trevor Warner, Dwayne Waltower, and Gary Russell, you all played crucial roles in my development as an athlete and person.

Lastly, a huge thank you to a friend who was taken far too soon. My friend, teammate, and most importantly a great human being, Billy Brown Jr. You are in our thoughts every day.

CONTENTS

INTRODUCTION

WE'VE SEEN IT plastered all over social media in the sports community for years. "I am blessed to announce my decision to continue my academic and athletic career at the University of…" The title of this book is inspired by the numerous young men and women across the country earning scholarships to compete in collegiate athletics each day. The sad reality is that many of these athletes will not finish with their degree; in fact, they may never step on the field. Even further, most athletes won't ever be given the opportunity to compete at the collegiate level. These athletes many times are not lacking in talent. There are many different reasons athletes don't make it. A lack of support, academic struggles, a poor decision off the field, a career-ending injury, financial struggles, and mental health break-downs are some of the more common reasons.

One fourth of all collegiate football players are first-generation college students. Furthermore, the athlete's whose parents did attend college wouldn't have done so in the last eighteen years. Most freshmen entering college are doing so in an entirely new environment. The intention of this book is to offer a unique and current perspective on the complete student-athlete experience from high-school recruitment through college graduation. There are several components of being a collegiate athlete that are never properly explained to young athletes during their growth and progression through school. Athletes find themselves worried about the jersey colors, campus location, and quality of parties before they grasp the harsh, demanding realities of being a college athlete. Many athletes are then placed into a "Sink or Swim" situation from their first day on campus. Between your mindset, mental health, finances, training, academics, team culture and leadership, time management, and campus life you will have to figure out how to adapt and succeed. This book will combine anecdotal stories, advice, and research aspiring to improve collegiate athletes' graduation rates, while also giving athletes the necessary knowledge to reach their full potential. I have unfortunately witnessed too many teammates end up incarcerated or unemployed after dropping out of school. At the Division I level, over one fifth of football players won't graduate. At the Division II level? One out of every two players will not finish their degree. It is an absolute waste of athletic talent and bright academic minds. I never want another young athlete to experience the same fate.

The format of this book will provide relatable experiences of my journey through high school, junior college, and the NCAA, as well as highlighting some of my former teammate's accomplishments and stories. Each chapter will contain real stories, facts, and practical, applicable advice that can be implemented in young athletes immediately and carried through their senior year of college. My goal is to make it so less kids endure struggle and are blindsided by situations as they go through school. My vision is for all athletes that aspire to compete at the collegiate level to be able to fulfill their maximum potential. The guidance in this book will help support athletes on their journey to athletic and academic success.

ABOUT THE AUTHOR

ANDREW CAPIRCHIO WAS born and raised in Fountain
Hills, Arizona, a suburb of the Phoenix metro area.
Growing up with three brothers and playing sports his
entire childhood, he was always very competitive and
result-driven. Andrew excelled in school at a young age,
where the decision was made to move him directly to 2nd
grade after finishing Kindergarten. Andrew was always
the physically smallest student in his grade up until
his sophomore year of high school. He didn't let that
dictate his plan for athletic success. While competing
in football, wrestling, and track, Andrew became one
of the most accomplished athletes in his high school's
history, setting seven school records in football and
earning 1st Team All-State Honors. In wrestling, he
secured a varsity spot four consecutive years, finishing
2nd in the state as a senior. Andrew was respected as a

leader on campus and in the community, being selected team captain of both squads. After graduation, Andrew turned down a few smaller partial scholarships to NAIA schools and decided to walk on to the local Scottsdale Community College football team. Andrew was a part of one of the most successful teams in school history his freshman season, finishing 10-1 as Valley of the Sun Bowl Champions. After battling injuries and adversity over three years, Andrew ended up leaving Scottsdale Community College as a starter and two-time Valley of the Sun Bowl Champion.

After transferring, Andrew graduated Summa Cum Laude (Sociology B.A) from Concordia University-St. Paul where he was Team Captain and a two-year starter for the Division II football program. Andrew currently works for Minneapolis Public Schools as a program coordinator for after-school care. In his free time Andrew also coaches youth football for Minneapolis Parks and Recreation as a volunteer. His love of football motivated his involvement in a non-profit in East St Paul, where he helps prepare athletes to advance to the collegiate level. The unique journey of being a junior college walk-on to Division II graduate exposed Andrew to plenty of unexpected challenges and hurdles. Throughout the course of his career Andrew had the opportunity to play with hundreds of teammates. Many of them transferred to universities all around the country at all divisions. A handful worked hard enough to have opportunities in the NFL and at various professional levels. Andrew's experiences as an athlete inspired him to write about his story, with hopes of supporting the thousands of young athletes who are in the same position he was years ago, clueless but hungry for success.

1
MINDSET

OFTENTIMES IN THE world of sports, you will hear expressions such as "They're a natural," or "You can't teach that, that's God-given talent!" These expressions simply diminish and downplay the characteristics that led to that athlete's success. As a society, we tend to look for reasons to justify others' success as a means of excusing our failures or relative lack of success. If someone has more talent than you, it is a reasonable belief to never expect to reach their status. This mindset could not be further from the truth, and any successful athlete will tell you a different story. Behind every All-American there is a story. A story that deserves to be told beyond their "freakish athletic ability." There are countless examples of the underdog coming out on top in the sports world. We've seen elite athletes overcoming their genetic shortcomings and adverse experiences when reaching their respective pinnacles. From a young age, as observational learners, athletes of all ages can see with their own eyes the results of hard work and a persistent mindset. Every team has the player who simply refuses to lose in drills, never gets outworked in the weight room or during conditioning, and always strives for greatness.

This isn't exactly groundbreaking news, nor is it always telling that those players will go on to college and become accomplished performers. This section of the book will identify a couple of specific character traits that I've witnessed in every successful athlete at the college level. Your mindset is entirely under your control, which is why this is the first area of focus. After reading this chapter, my hope is for you to immediately implement these three traits into your daily habits, not only as an athlete, but as a person. You can make the conscious decision to either commit to earning your dream scholarship, or be the person on the couch talking about how they wish they had stuck with it. The choice is yours.

Perseverance — Every athlete and every person will encounter adversity at various points throughout their life. The response is ultimately what is indicative of how adversity affects each person. Think of your favorite athlete. Look up their career and story, and you will see they experienced injuries, setbacks, and unfortunate circumstances. Every athlete who didn't make it to the top likely experienced these same events. What separates the two? Successful athletes appear to carry an innate response to not flinch or waver in the face of adversity. This response is due to using adversity as motivation to return to play, in hopes of dominating more than they were previously. There are several examples of adversity you may face during your athletic career, including injuries, family hardship, financial hardship, mental health issues (self-doubt, anxiety, depression) to name a few. Let's focus on the most common and widely-occurring setback—injuries.

Great athletes look at injuries as an opportunity to bounce back stronger. They never skip a therapy session, and they never jeopardize their recovery process with poor decisions. Great athletes possess the uncanny ability to have an unbreakable faith in their situation no matter how dire their circumstances may be. Their passion for their sport and love for competition outweighs any personal issues. This is not intended to describe the successful athlete as a robot incapable of feeling emotion. These athletes hurt, cry, and struggle just as much as any other human going through a crisis. The difference is in the attitude of response and action with a lack of doubt. Nowhere during the trials of adversity do elite athletes consider their sport to be the root cause of their problems, and in turn consider quitting or giving up. They understand that taking the easy way out will not erase their problems. These athletes rarely feel sorry for themselves or view themselves as a victim of their circumstances.

I will share my personal experiences with injuries as an athlete. Through my athletic career, I suffered an incredibly bizarre string of injuries that sidelined me at very inopportune times. I witnessed many other players suffer the same unfortunate fate. Never once did I consider quitting or giving up. I showed up to the training room or physical therapy office every day with the belief that I was getting better. These injuries were simply speed bumps in the road to my destination.

During my freshman season, I was strictly a special team's player. I was a seventeen-year-old kid competing against grown men who had transferred from some of the most prestigious schools in the country. Since I was a walk-on and physically underdeveloped player, making the team and travel roster was an accomplishment for my first season. I will never forget one moment lining up at corner on punt return that season. I was no more than 5'9" and 175 pounds. We were playing Arizona Western and their punt gunner came out, a top-ranked safety with fifteen plus Division I offers. Off the snap, the gunner made one quick move nearly causing me to fall on my ass before burning me down the field. Every athlete has experienced this feeling. It's what I call an "Oh shit" moment. Whether it is just based off your matchup, or you made a mistake during the play, or you forgot to bring your helmet to the game, every athlete has experienced that nervous feeling in their stomach of realizing you messed up. The best athletes learn to eliminate these moments from their thought processes early on. My coach gave me an earful on the sideline, as I'm sure it seemed I wasn't even trying during that play from his perspective. Of course, I had given my best effort during the play, but my mindset was inexperienced. These are the moments I am able to look back at and laugh about. There is no doubt in my mind as that gunner lined up across me before the snap, he could see my lack of confidence. I had lost that play long before the ball was snapped. The only reason I even knew he had those offers was because I had spent time researching the highlights of players whose level of play I aspired to reach. Had I never known who he was, he would have been no different than any other athlete. It was not uncommon for me to get exposed by superior athletes as a freshman. Losing reps at practice, struggling to compete, and straight up failing were standard on the daily. I'm sure this is a feeling many athletes can relate to early in their careers. I was outmatched both physically and skill-wise. However, more importantly, my effort never changed throughout these failures. I was always trying to learn and become a better player. I stayed on the field every night after practice putting in extra work, sometimes after the lights had long been turned off. I kept my head on straight and trusted the process. Many times, freshmen will struggle to transition as quickly as they imagined they would. Everyone goes from being the best player in their high school program to competing with players who have three or four years of experience on them. Little did I know my freshman fall semester would be my only healthy semester ever as a collegiate athlete.

Heading into my second season I had the goal of starting. You only get two seasons at junior college, so one would hope this is every man on the roster's goal. I never missed a single workout or practice during the offseason, and I felt prepared to compete. Heading into my sophomore season I was dealing with chronic patellar tendonitis. This is a common injury, but my specific case had me struggling to walk around or even perform a bodyweight squat. We tried everything in the training room. One of the more memorable treatment attempts included our athletic trainer grabbing this huge, ceramic, phallic-shaped object. He would then proceed to roll my shorts up into my crotch and put a healthy portion of cocoa butter on my legs. For the next 15 minutes, some of the worst pain of my life ensued as he dug the tool into my quads. The girls' soccer team always sat and laughed as I lay there writhing around on the training table. It may have looked like a torture scene from a low budget film, and unfortunately it didn't even get rid of my knee pain. I eventually made the decision to redshirt after missing half the season. I went to physical therapy for eight weeks after the season before my knees felt comfortable enough to perform football movements.

During spring workouts of that same year, I was competing in an agility workout on the field during team workouts. I felt a pop in my groin and knew something was wrong. There wasn't time for me to be injured, as I was already on the border of roster cuts for spring football. I participated in a few spring practices through excruciating pain. After the first spring practice I was told by my defensive back's coach that my name was one of the first discussed for being cut from the team. My position coach told me he was fighting for me, but it was ultimately the head coach's decision. I knew if I missed practice for a less than surgical injury I would be cut from the team, no questions asked. I tried my best to compete until enough was enough. I remember running during one practice and feeling extremely slow. A few of my teammates and coaches were commenting on how unathletic I looked. At this point, the pain was unbearable and there was no chance for me to seriously compete. I went to the doctor and was diagnosed with a grade-III osteitis pubis injury. This is an uncommon sports injury, and not typical of football particularly. Essentially, my pubic bone was severely inflamed, and the tendons were tearing from the bone on a micro level. I missed the entire remaining spring football season and endured another two months of physical therapy to prepare me for summer training.

After a successful summer of busting my ass at work, on the field, and in the weight room, I was finally healthy heading into fall camp of my redshirt sophomore season. I had been practicing as the starting corner. The head coach walked past me on the field near the end of a summer workout and said, "God damnit, Cap you've made some real progress. There's actually a chance you might play for us this year." You couldn't wipe the smile off my face with a right hook. In our first fall camp scrimmage, we were playing Eastern Arizona, a triple option team. The first play of the game they came to my side of the field with a toss to the runningback, I broke on it and made a solid tackle for a loss in the backfield. As I lowered to make the tackle, though, I slipped awkwardly in a muddy spot on the field. There was a pop, and I immediately knew I was injured once again. I was screaming every profanity as loud as I could in the back of my mind. In the morning, my hamstring was swollen with about two inches of fluid and was entirely black and blue–it was a pulled hamstring. I missed the rest of fall camp and our first two games of the season in my new second home, the training room. The third game of the season

I stepped on to the field for my first play of the season, back on good old special teams–kickoff return. I was holding a block in the middle of the field when a lineman collapsed into my knee from the side. I heard and felt a crunch and dropped immediately. At that moment, I thought it may have been the end of my career. This occurred on the very first play I returned from my hamstring injury. I absolutely couldn't believe it. I remember my girlfriend explaining to me after the game how furious my dad was in the stands at the game. He was probably tired of coughing up $5 to watch me sit on the sideline every Saturday night. I got an MRI and had an MCL sprain in my knee. I missed four more weeks of the season. Once I was healthy enough to return, there was only four more weeks of regular season remaining.

Let's recap. I was now at the point where I had been in college football for two and a half seasons and had never stepped on the field for a defensive snap. This is incredibly rare at the junior college level. In fact, I challenge you to find someone with a similar experience. During this time, several of my teammates quit, plenty transferred, and a ton more got cut. I never lost sight of my end goal: I was set on graduating college a football player. I showed up to every single weight session, every single meeting, and never once complained or asked for anything. I persevered, but it didn't feel like it at the time. I was so confident in the work I had put in, I was convinced the result would be what I wanted. Essentially, I was just going through the days the same way I always had. The seventh game of our season rolled around, and I got my first start due to the starter being arrested on Thursday. It wasn't the way I envisioned getting my opportunity, but I could not have cared less. I was ready, and I ended up playing well, recording my first and only career sack that game. Going into the next week I had earned an opportunity to start at a different position due to a change in our defensive scheme. I ended up starting the rest of the season and playing well, with our team winning every game. We secured the rights to host the Valley of the Sun Bowl, we were set to face Central Lakes College from Minnesota. Practicing all the way up to December, I had three or four scouts from NAIA and Division II schools interested in watching me play in the bowl game. I got mononucleosis (commonly known as mono) the week before the game. You can't make this stuff up. This virus enlarges your spleen and makes it life-threatening to compete in a contact sport. Just like that, my junior college career came to an unexpected end, and with no scholarship offers my football career was foreseeably finished.

I graduated in December and began emailing schools like crazy for a shot to transfer in the fall. In the meantime, I was painting houses full time in Arizona and training on my own. Things were very quiet for several months. In April, I eventually got a call from Concordia-St. Paul's defensive coordinator and with it he offered a very solid scholarship. I began to cry after getting off the phone. I ended up committing the day after my official visit. I had seen the light at the end of the tunnel. Often people hear about my junior college journey and are surprised I stuck with it. Balancing school, work, football, and a social life is never easy, add to the fact I was a relatively unsuccessful athlete, it made the journey that much more difficult and frustrating at times. I always respond and tell them that I knew I would make it. It wasn't a matter of other people believing in me or seeing it, I had already convinced myself that every ounce of work I put in from my freshman year of high school would pay off. My story is one of a thousand like it. I have seen teammates overcome much more dire circumstances than myself. Multiple ACL surgeries, being cut from a team and transferring to another, etc. The ability to persevere tirelessly through the challenges of being a college athlete makes the journey that much more achievable.

One of the distinct differences between the mindset of successful athletes and the less successful ones, is the idea that the trait of perseverance is never in doubt. It may even come across as an innate ability or sense of faith: that there simply was no existing option of failure. The idea that your path is one entirely paved by yourself is a trait that will carry you through any challenge in life, long after your playing days are over. The easy decision is to quit once you get injured. It doesn't come as a surprise to learn that former collegiate athletes rank higher than their non-athlete counterparts in purposeful well-being after graduation. Student-athlete graduates are motivated to achieve their goals and enjoy what they do each day, proven by their track record during college. The perseverance of student athletes allows them to pursue passions and interests that are meaningful and important. No number of setbacks will stop the pursuit of these important goals. The struggles of collegiate athletics build resilience that translates once you're playing days are over. However, if you take the path of least resistance, you are developing habits that can severely hinder your opportunities for success later. Don't quit once you have an injury. Forget the idea of transferring if you can't secure a starting position. Pick up a second job when you can't afford to eat. Accepting the challenges head on and pushing through will only lead you to new levels of growth.

Vision – Every single action requires an intent. This intent needs to be focused and directed at the long-term goal of the individual. The ability to see the larger vision and make decisions that reflect that vision is vital to reaching the aspired level of success. The word vision here is not referring to sight, although good eyesight is equally important in the world of athletics. Vision in this usage is referring to the ability to keep the end-goal in perspective at all times, which is graduating with a college degree. Successful people and successful athletes practice making choices throughout the day with a tireless intent to achieve their goals. This may sound dramatic, but it is extremely practical and applicable. What food are you grabbing in the cafeteria, and are you reading the nutrition labels? Are you attending the voluntary workouts, or staying home and playing video games? Are you skipping out on watching film of your upcoming opponent to watch Netflix? These are real examples of choices among countless others that athletes make on a daily basis. The great ones don't have to think hard or long about these choices. The decisions were made before the question was answered, this is a character trait that is developed. In the weight room, I used to consciously decide which arm I picked up loose weights with to ensure I wasn't working one side of my body harder than the other. That may sound absolutely insane to many people reading this. I challenge you to think back through the current week, and spend some time reflecting on your own decisions. What did you eat? When did you fall asleep? How did you use your free time? The list of questions is endless and always changing. The idea is that during every waking second of your day, your thoughts and actions are done for a valued reason. These reasons vary from individual to individual, yet the habit becomes second nature. Many athletes may wander through their day, enjoying their free time taking naps or playing Madden. They may walk into class five minutes late, wearing their headphones while slumping their head on their desk. In order to reach the level of success every athlete strives for, those poor choices aren't sustainable. Every decision needs to be made with the vision of the team's success.

To quote my former head coach at Scottsdale Community College, Doug Madoski, "Don't do anything this weekend to hurt yourself, your family, or this football team." When a coach says this, there are certain players they don't have to worry about—they know they are always making the right decisions. Strive to be a player that the coach is able to count on due to your vision of success. I remember in high school when I expressed to my teammates or friends that I wanted to play in college, I usually got laughed at. Some of my own friends flat out told me to my face that it would never happen. I was too small, too slow, not strong enough, there was always an abundance of reasons why. At my former high school, the graduation always takes place at a local park surrounding a lake with a fountain. All the seniors bus over from the high school to the park. Groups are let off at the sidewalk to walk down into the theatre seating, surrounded by friends and family. As I was lined up and prepared to walk down for my high school graduation, my varsity defensive coordinator approached me. We made small talk, and he eventually asked what my plans were for next year. I told him that I planned to walk on at a community college to continue playing. His verbatim response was, "You know, everyone has to hang up the cleats sometime." I will never forget that moment. With a strong vision, negative comments don't get taken to heart. They are simply excused.

One display of vision I could never forget occurred during my freshman season. Our team was riding the bus to an away game. I was sitting next to one of my former teammate's, defensive lineman Siupeli Anau. We were driving past the Arizona Cardinals stadium in Glendale, and Peli, as we referred to him, looked me dead in my eyes and said, "I'm going to be playing there in two years, Cap." I didn't doubt Peli at all–in fact, I was motivated by his confidence in himself. Something about the way Peli said it made everyone believe him, it wasn't the words that mattered, it was his attitude. The exchange left a strong impact on me as a freshman. Peli was a local Arizona player that was an undersized, walk-on defensive lineman. He left Scottsdale Community College as a first-team all-conference performer and our team defensive MVP. He ended up transferring to Northern Arizona University and having a successful junior year, earning Honorable Mention Big-Sky. He suffered a season-ending injury as a senior and returned for one more season after a medical redshirt. He finished his collegiate career earning First-Team All Big-Sky honors and was signed as an undrafted free agent to who else but the Arizona Cardinals. Sure enough, Peli was playing in the Cardinals stadium just like he'd said. Peli was imperfect as an athlete just like the rest of us. The fact that Peli is still playing professional football speaks to the fact his vision was consistent and paired with an undeniable desire. Season-ending injuries, off-the-field adversity, being a walk-on, playing Division IA, none of those events took away Peli's vision of becoming an NFL player. The only thing that would prevent Peli from reaching that stage was himself, and he understood that everyday when he went to work.

Where did other players lack in vision? Teammates with multiple Division I offers playing pool in the student center while their class was in session wasn't uncommon. There were instances of a lack of judgement where teammates were getting involved in criminal acts off the field, or getting in fights during class. There are countless scenarios. There is also a lack of preparation or explanation for athletes' transition to college to help guide their decision-making process. A lot of athletes have the vision of where they want to go, but not the skill or knowledge of how to make the correct decisions to get there. Getting in a fight in high school and college will have entirely different consequences. It is that way with just about every decision. In college you are on a contract through your school and coach, and most likely any slip up or error of judgement could be punishable by release from the team. Whether it is one crucial mistake, or thousands of unrecognizable mistakes, a lack of vision can setback any athlete's career. Later on in the book we will discuss strategies and give advice to help guide young athletes decision making and preparation to best execute their vision.

Competitiveness – One of my most vivid memories from youth football occurred while walking with my mother to her car after the game. My team had completely dominated and went on to an uncontested shutout victory. I was extremely frustrated and crying like a baby. My mom was extremely confused so she asked me, "What's wrong? You guys won and you played great so, why are you crying?"

My response was: "Winning like that isn't fun." I had legitimately been upset because the game was not competitive.

One of my former teammates used to wear a flashy gold watch at practice. When he was asked why he wore it, he would respond "Because time is the only thing that can stop me." Shaquan Curenton, who we referred to as Shaq, was one of the most frustrating wide receivers I ever had the chance to compete with in college. His competitiveness was next level. He would talk smack, and back it up every single day. Shaq always wanted to face the best defensive back on the opposing team. Nothing else mattered to him except for winning. But he didn't want to win only during the big moments. He wanted to win every single repetition, regardless of the environment. Whether he was helping on scout team or catching the game-winning touchdown on Saturday, he was always going full speed. This is a direct result of the amount of pride and passion he played with. He was constantly heard shouting, "Not between the white lines" at practice. Meaning, it didn't matter how close of a bond you had off the field, he wanted to kick your ass while in practice or a game. That was his intent. Shaq wasn't born with a different mindset or unattainable physical tools. He wanted to make you look silly, because he wanted to succeed. He wanted to succeed because he had his own personal motivation. Everyone can decide to find that motivation within themselves, everyone has that capability. In my experience, players like Shaq are often the cause of a lot of frustration amongst opposing players. There is no doubt in my mind Shaq made me and everyone else around him a better player. Whether you appreciated his smack talk and confidence or not, he brought out the best in you as a competitor.

Athletes are required to dedicate so much time and energy to their sport each week. An uncompetitive blowout victory on Saturday doesn't create the same taste of accomplishment as a hard-fought win. Great athletes carry this attitude with them throughout life even after sports. Great athletes don't settle for a career that doesn't challenge them. They may pursue graduate school, coaching, teaching, or a finance position. Whatever it may be, you can be assured they will continue to climb and stretch their limits. Great athletes should hate dominating. If you are dominating, you are not competing; if you are not competing, you are not getting better. I often thrived while I was the underdog, and often underperformed when I was considered the favorite. My mindset was different if I was expected to lose. Competitors win. Competitors win in life, and competitors win in sports. There is an intangible aspect of playing sports that brings out a different emotion in people. Those who can harness this emotion and turn it into a borderline obsessive desire to improve continually create unbelievable success stories. You may have heard the expression "I hated losing more than I enjoyed winning." This expression is within the blood flow of winners.

The summer before I was headed to Minnesota, I was preparing for my upcoming season with one of my best friends and former teammates, Jamar Pinnock, and his trainer. This trainer works with first-round NFL draft prospects every year. The trainer only worked with athletes he specifically invited, however Jamar didn't have a car at the time, and I was providing him a ride. We were at this hill in the desert running sprints up it. It had no trail, it was just a hill in the middle of the desert with rocks, cacti, and bushes on it. Jamar is a physical specimen to look at, standing 6'3" and carrying 230 pounds of muscle mass. Jamar was also a starter at the Division IAA level. This happened to be my first experience with this trainer and the hill. On our third repetition going up and down, I beat Jamar down the hill. The trainer started screaming at Jamar and said, "You let a f*cking new guy beat you!" and he threw his stop watch into the bushes, got into his car, and drove off. Never in my life had I felt so disrespected. The reason I beat Jamar down that hill was because I competed. This didn't mean Jamar wasn't trying or had given up– I simply got the better of him on that run. I wasn't about to put forth poor effort for any reason ever. This trainer felt that was a reason to discredit the work I had put in. He later texted Jamar and told him I wasn't welcome to the workouts anymore due to the fact I wasn't paying.

After I arrived in Minnesota, the first day of fall camp consisted of running the conditioning test. I hadn't known what the test would be composed of, so I hadn't prepared for it at all during the summer. If you failed the conditioning test, you were required to do extra conditioning a few days a week at 5:30 in the morning before practice during fall camp. No sir. I was not about to be in that club. The defensive back group had to run three sets of 90-yard sprints in a certain time with timed rest periods of ten seconds. You could miss the specified time once and still pass. The very first repetition of the conditioning test I ran 80 yards and stopped. Being a new player, no one knew my name yet or they just didn't care to alert me, and I stood there until the timer beeped. I used my one freebie on the very first repetition. It wasn't the best start, but I was alive. By the third set, there were only three defensive backs left. The last repetition of the test, myself and one other defensive back were headed stride for stride for the finish line, feeding off of each other's energy. We both passed the finish line simultaneously. It is no coincidence that player turned out to be one of my closest friends and teammates, Brian Szutkowski. Brian was one of the hardest working and most competitive teammates I had the pleasure of playing with. This competitive edge is what keeps players in programs that may be having a transition year, the competitor's nature is to try get the program back on track, instead of transferring to a school that is winning in that moment.

Any successful athlete's mindset toward competitiveness could be summed up in a quote from my favorite actor, Will Smith: "The only thing that I see that is distinctly different about me is I'm not afraid to die on a treadmill. Right? I will not be out-worked, period. You might have more talent than me, you might be smarter than me, you might be sexier than me, you might be all of those things, you got it on me in nine categories. But if we get on the treadmill together, right, there's two things: You're getting off first, or I'm going to die. It's really that simple, right?"

One of my former teammates, Craig Kanyangarara, was a true leader. Not only for his performance on the field, but his champion mindset and ability to push others toward greatness. Craig overcame struggles of his own during his athletic career, originally travelling to the United States from Zimbabwe as a teenager having limited knowledge of the game. Craig landed a spot at Scottsdale Community College the same season I enrolled. During my time at Scottsdale, Craig was a player who simply never stopped. He never stopped giving maximum effort, he never stopped competing, he never stopped excelling, and he never stopped dreaming. After an unorthodox journey, Craig eventually landed at the University of Alabama Birmingham on full scholarship. He recently graduated and was awarded the "Changing the Narrative" award by Rachel Baribeau for his aspirations to make an impact off the field. I asked Craig to share some of his perspective as an athlete and his thoughts toward what creates the mindset of a great athlete. He has this to share:

"Making it to college is not easy by any means and when you make it in, it gets even harder. It becomes even more difficult if you plan on having an above-average, or great, career in sports, academics, or hopefully both. It will require a great amount of self-discipline in order to take care of your business. Not everyone is fortunate enough to receive a scholarship or financial assistance, so you might have to pick up a job or two. Most athletes enter college fresh out of high school between the ages of seventeen and nineteen, or you might be coming from a junior college and be a few years older before you enter a university. What I'm trying to say is most of us enter college young-minded and inexperienced, which is understandable, because you are. However, you must mature very quickly, because you are entering into the early stages of your adulthood. What you sow in your early years you will reap in your later years.

The first thing you have to ask yourself is what do you want to do with your life? Also, you must find your why–what motivates you to achieve your goals and aspirations? Because there are going to be times when you have to pick up two or even three jobs to support yourself and your family, or pay for your education. When you don't want to go to class what's going to get you out of bed? When a coach gets in your face, what will make you hold your composure? When you're not getting as many opportunities as you'd hoped, what's going to motivate you to put in the extra work? Are you willing to rush to work after class and stay up studying after a long day? It has to matter to you, unless you want to be average or at the bottom. It's necessary to know what motivates you, because you have to constantly make small choices that can have a major impact on your life or career. You have to be mentally tough to make some of those choices and decisions. Mental toughness is not just the ability to withstand a lot of pain, it could be not smoking weed, knowing you could be selected for a random drug test. It could also be waking up early, not going out, saving money, and so on. These decisions, which I don't like calling sacrifices–but rather actions, will impact your dream, so you have to make the right decisions.

Hold yourself accountable. I had to learn the hard way that no one is going to do shit for you. You will have to make a way for yourself, because once you are in college you are on your own. You're legally considered an adult, and the choices you make are extremely important. Don't be afraid to dream big. Once you've dreamt it, create long- and short-term goals. The next step is to have a plan on how you will accomplish your goals. Most importantly, have faith and stay positive along your journey. It's going to get rough at times–it's not easy by any means. The harder my journey became, the more I got closer to God and started working on my faith. You can't do it alone, seek God and ask for help. Focus on what you can control. Faith will help you in areas you can't control. You can't worry or stress about everything, this will destroy your dreams as an athlete. Understand that adversity will reveal what kind of person you truly are. No matter what the circumstances, you must stay positive and continue to work smarter and harder toward what you control. You don't have to always go hard. Sometimes you might have to rest or take a break. Have balance; all athletes practice this, especially the greats. It's okay to go push yourself, but you must take care of your body and mind in order to perform at the highest level. God Bless, good luck, stay positive, and conquer your dreams.

2
RECRUITING

WHETHER IT'S THE Instagram pictures with jerseys, or the three-minute video clips on Twitter announcing commitments, every athlete has seen it. The recruiting process is getting flashier and flashier, leading athletes to fall in love with the process of getting recruited even more than actually being an athlete. Recruiting is an essential part of the journey. Without recruiting there is no signing day for high school or junior college athletes. There is important information to realize while going through the process. You should start the recruiting process as early as you have realistic marketable film. Younger athletes can learn and gain valuable knowledge in this chapter, but should be focusing on their personal sport for the time being. Conversely, the recruiting process can teach valuable skills and lessons that translate into other areas of life. We will explore options for playing after high school, how to sell yourself and get exposure, highlight video and coach contact advice, and things to consider when choosing a school. The recruiting process can be an emotionally draining ride, from the excitement of getting your first letters, to the possible disappointment of coaching changes and offers being pulled last minute. There are several components of the process, and it is best to get as much assistance as possible from your coaches and parents if at all possible. Before diving into specifics, be forewarned there are several recruiting services available. Some of these services offer legitimate exposure, while others are a waste of resources and time. Investigate heavily if you decide to utilize a paid service, while keeping in mind that any athlete can handle the recruiting process themselves just as effectively with the correct knowledge.

A. Options

If you are reading this, chances are you are in the chunk of high school or college athletes that do not currently have big-time Division I scholarship offers. Most high school athletes do not have any recruiting attention at all. While it is never too late to pursue playing college football, the recruiting process is best started as early as possible. There are several routes to pursue playing football after high school.

1. **Signing with an NCAA or NAIA program**. This is the most commonly pursued method and most common way of advancing to the next level for high-school athletes. This is where you sign on national signing day of your senior year committing on a scholarship offer to play for a NCAA I/II/NAIA university. NCAA Division III athletes sign an offer sheet, although their scholarship offer cannot be bound to

athletics, usually receiving financial aid packages in the form of grants and academic scholarships. Signing with an NCAA or NAIA program out of high school offers you the opportunity to go to a school of your choice for four or five years and stay in one place to accomplish your goals. If you are lucky you will have the same coaching staff your entire career, and enjoy the college athlete experience while going on to earn your degree. This route avoids having to transfer or enroll in a two-year school. Your scholarship will typically be guaranteed year to year, assuming you do not breach your contract to get kicked off the team or expelled from the school. There are large variances between each division of college football and very different football, academic, and campus experiences. Every high school athlete aspires to play Division I football. Sold-out crowds, large stadiums, an unnecessary supply of gear, and traveling by plane. The reality of the situation is, significantly more players will sign partial scholarships to lower division schools. The division of the institution you attend does not determine your experience. I have heard several stories from teammates and their friends who transferred from Division I schools, to have better experiences at smaller schools due to unforeseeable circumstances. Do not knock a lower-division school; instead, evaluate the academics available for your desires, your financial situation and the aid offered, and your impression of the college as a complete package. If you utilize the correct resources and ask the proper questions during the recruiting process you will feel extremely comfortable with the school you decide to attend. You should have already visited the school, identified an area of interest for a major, and come to terms you will be living in the town for four or five years. If you don't sign with a NCAA/ NAIA school during your senior year, fear not, there are more options.

2. **Signing with a junior college program**. This is a route less pursued, yet still offers tons of opportunities for student athletes in several different sports to continue playing at the next level. Junior colleges can offer scholarships in some conferences, and others cannot. There is usually a strong balance of scholarship and walk-on players at this level. Junior colleges do not have a travel budget for recruiting, they don't host camps, and they rely primarily on social media and the internet for recruiting purposes. Most teams will offer walk-on tryouts right before the season and accept several players. A lot of junior colleges will not have on-campus housing, and are typically low enrollment small campuses. The facilities are usually less flashy in comparison to respective NCAA programs. Junior colleges offer student athletes the ability to play for one or two seasons before transferring to a four-year program. Junior colleges are significantly less expensive than universities and can offer opportunities for athletes who are under-recruited or under-developed coming out of high school. Athletes that only have Division II offers, but feel like they are a Division I athlete, may decide to go to a junior college for developmental reasons, as well as athletes with no offers at all who are

trying to continue their dream. You also see Division I transfers who need to bridge a year before moving to another school. Another scenario would be athletes who do not academically qualify out of high school. Athletes who do qualify can transfer at any time from a junior college to a four-year program. Athletes who did not qualify will have to earn their two-year associate's degree before transferring.

I have played with teammates from each of the respective backgrounds. Players with no offers out of high school who signed Division I after a few years. Players who bounced back from a Division I program and signed with a lower-level program. Players who didn't qualify academically and improved their academics to transfer to a university. Junior college is a melting pot of athletes from countless different backgrounds. The biggest difference between junior college football and four-year football is the environment of the program and campus. Everyone at a junior college is there for one reason: to get out. There is certainly still a sense of school pride and desire for team success, although not typically comparable with a university. Every player in junior college is competing for a better opportunity, though whether it comes along with team success or relationships, may or may not be important to them. Coaches have less invested in the players that were not recruited heavily, so don't take it personally if a player gets brought in two weeks before the season to land right on top of you on the depth chart. It's a business. Heading into my redshirt sophomore season, we had a defensive back transfer in from the University of

Texas less than a few weeks before our first game. I had been in the program for years, and he entered in with a starting spot essentially guaranteed. I was not bitter; I understood the reality of the situation. Rather, I was excited to be able to compete with another great athlete. Junior college is a different beast when it comes to internal team competition due to the nature of the circumstances. You must be willing to put in work and make sacrifices to transfer out of junior college football.

3. **Walking on to a NCAA or junior college program**. Walking on to a program is trying out for a school to earn a position on their football team with no scholarship money. This is an option for players who truly love the sport and are not focused on being the star of the team. Most walk-on players become scout-team players for a large duration of their career, and they may never appear in a meaningful game. This is all while paying for school out of pocket. Of course, you get the experience of being a part of a college football team, access to all the team's facilities and academic support, and the campus experience. There are a handful of walk-ons each year that go on to play significant roles on their team, and even fewer make it to the NFL. Any athlete considering walking on will have to seriously look in the mirror and ask themselves how important playing college football is to them. Walking on at a junior college offers a higher chance of playing in comparison to walking on at a Division I university. However, walking on at a Division I school

offers benefits of being a part of a strong alumni base, networking, and a well-known branded degree.

I don't advise walking on at a school in most scenarios. The exception is if the athlete is heavily educated on the expectations and reality of the role, and the right opportunity presents itself. There is a distinct difference between walk-on players and scholarship players at the Division I level, and there's even a noticeable impact at the lower divisions. Just be prepared to work harder then everyone else. Paying your dues as a scout team player, in the weight room, and in the classroom for a fraction of the glory.

4. **Taking a year off.** This is the most difficult, and least-pursued option available. However, I have personally seen it work in favor for several of my former teammates. There are many reasons why someone may take a gap year after high school before entering college. Travelling, saving money, volunteering, searching for an academic interest, etc. In the case of athletes, it is most commonly to train and develop physically, or to save money to pursue a specific school. I graduated high school three months after I turned seventeen. I may have benefited from a year off to develop physically and mature before entering college football, but I just as well may have never regained the motivation to pursue it. This decision is a difficult one and will vary on a case to case basis.

It is not recommended for a few reasons. The further you are away from school, meaning time you've spent apart from it, the more difficult it is to maintain the motivation to advance. Quite similarly, the longer you are away from playing contact football the more difficult it is to maintain true game speed and instinct. This isn't to say this is not an option. You may have had a scholarship pulled last minute, you may have never received a scholarship, or simply you might have had a change of heart after being away from the game. One of my teammates from Scottsdale Community College, DJ Olmstead, was away from the game for a couple of years before walking on to Scottsdale Community College. He ended up earning a starting spot along with a full-ride scholarship to the University of Idaho. DJ finished his career as a First Team All-American at Washburn University. I am grateful to have had the opportunity to play with DJ; he truly was a leader and teammate who brought out the best in everyone around him. He never allowed an opportunity to question his character, motives, or drive. These are a few reasons he was able to succeed at a high level after being away from the game. DJ was drafted in the inaugural draft for the professional Alliance of American Football. If you can harness the qualities of a winner, you will find a way to make it happen, no matter how long or arduous the process may be.

In regard to deciding which route is best to take after high-school there is an extremely important topic to discuss- eligibility. Your eligibility begins at the Division I level the second you enroll in a school full-time. This is known as a running clock. If you enroll in fall of 2019, your eligibility is exhausted in the year 2024, regardless if you ever stepped on the field or not. You can drop out of school after your freshman year, and if you decide two years later you want to play, you will have lost those two years at the Division I level. However, if you attend school less than full-time, and never attended full-time, you are not exhausting any eligibility. There are redshirts and medical redshirts that add a year of eligibility as well. Eligibility impacts transferring in nearly every circumstance, which is something to consider. There are several components that go into the recruiting process that require educating yourself. When it comes to eligibility, there is no excuse to not understand how the process works. It is written in plain language on the NCAA website, so I encourage you to visit and investigate if you have any questions or concerns regarding your eligibility as an athlete. Moving forward with the recruiting process requires you to market yourself as a product, convincing college coaches of your value as an individual.

B. Selling yourself and gaining exposure.

You may be thinking, okay great! I understand what the options are for playing football after college, but I am currently a sophomore, junior, or senior in high school and I haven't been contacted by a single school. What do I do now? You may not even have a highlight tape developed. There are certain steps and actions to take to ensure you are getting as much exposure as possible during the recruiting process. College coaches never once visited my high school to recruit someone from my team. The responsibility lies on you alone to contact and communicate with schools. If you find yourself relying on a recruiting service, your high school coach, your parents, or your Twitter page to handle your recruitment, you will likely find yourself without a home come signing day. The process to getting recruited is simple when broken down:

- Play at a high level and develop a sought-after resumé (highlight plays, physical ability).

- Evaluate yourself internally and establish target schools. Are you a Division I, II, III, NAIA, or junior college player? Compare and contrast yourself to highlight videos and physical attributes of players at the level you aspire to play at. Get feedback from coaches at camps.

- Contact coaches consistently and follow up (emailing, texting, calling, social media, visiting coaches and camps- selling your content, otherwise known as getting exposure).

- Distinguish and identify serious interest (interpreting the recruiting process and coach communication).

- Schedule a few visits to top schools that have made an offer (evaluate future potential, gather perspective on school and campus life).

- Decide and commit to your new team (sign letter of intent and prepare to report).

The biggest downfall of the modern recruiting process is that athletes often get caught up in the pursuit of "status," rather than focusing on the product they are displaying. This pursuit of status is posted all over Twitter, Instagram, Facebook, and recruiting websites. Players are constantly posting pictures in jerseys on visits, posting snapchats of letters from coaches with captions of whatever song is currently trending. As an athlete, you must not lose sight of your goals in the attention of the recruiting process. Your primary focus should always be on your performance on the field and in the classroom. Recruiting only becomes a duty once you are putting forth maximum effort in the other necessary stages. There is instant gratification in displaying your photos on social media and receiving praise and likes from your network and community. However, if this doesn't translate into scholarship money in writing, you need to reevaluate your priorities. Simply put, there is a reason only a small percentage of athletes get the opportunity to go on to the next level. Not everyone is athletically and academically developed enough to compete at the collegiate level. Focus on being the absolute best football player you can be and making plays, first and foremost. If you are dedicating more time to the recruiting process than you are to winning a state championship, you need to look in the mirror. Don't ever lose the passion you carried for your sport as a young kid playing in the street or your backyard. Coaches are looking for athletes who bring value to their campus athletically, academically, and in the community.

Once you have built a positive reputation as a player and leader, you are going to want to develop a plan of action for how you want to contact schools and get yourself out there in front of coaches. In high school I wrote up a Microsoft Word document with a list of coaches from all the schools I was interested in playing for. I referred to this document to email and contact schools on a consistent basis. This process is easy, and there is no excuse to not accessing this information. Start by googling the school name followed by "athletic directory," simply scroll down and locate the football coach's school email addresses. Copy and paste the entire coaching staff's email addresses into the Word document, and repeat this method until you have gathered the contact information of every single school you may be interested in. I had several hundred coaches' emails in this file. In addition to the coaches' contact information, I researched the school's academic programs, level of competition, players of my position on their roster, where the school was located, how much tuition was, etc. Naturally this is all the information you should be looking for in a school, but it becomes even more important during the recruiting process. Do not bother wasting your own time or a coach's time in contacting schools you would not actually be willing to play at. This is the equivalent of interviewing for a job you wouldn't accept or going on a date with a person you are not actually interested in. Nothing is more frustrating than having your time wasted intentionally. It simply shows a lack of respect, and quite frankly you must remember there is always someone wanting to take your lunch money in the world of college football.

Before you begin contacting schools there are certain things you will want to have readily available in order for coaches to take you seriously:

- Highlight Tape (edited with marker on yourself, formatted properly, no music.)

- Vitals (height/weight/age/graduation year).

- Test Scores/GPA/Academic Interest (ACT/SAT scores as soon as they are available).

- If applicable, include a list of schools that have offered you scholarships.

- Eligibility for junior college recruits (when you are eligible to transfer, and how many years you have left to compete).

- Current Coach Contact Information/Personal Contact Information (secure a professional and reasonable email address). Do not include coach contact information if for any reason they would not positively endorse you as an athlete. You can't assume your coach will vouch for you simply because they are your coach. Have an honest conversation with your coach addressing your goals and ask for feedback.

Things to avoid including in communication with coaches:

- Questions about the campus or school that can be researched online (Example: How many students do you have?) This shows laziness on your part due to a lack of researching the school and program. It is the equivalent of showing up to a job interview and being unable to answer basic answers about the company.

- Under any circumstances, absolutely do not ever lie or fabricate statistics or vitals. This is a guaranteed way to get yourself removed from a team's recruiting list. It sounds ridiculous to even give this advice, but you would be surprised at how often this occurs. I think I claimed I ran a 4.59 forty-yard-dash on my highlight tape, which absolutely was not accurate when I was sixteen. I thought I would outsmart the college coaches and put it at 4.59, because 4.60 sounds too perfect. I figured I had cracked the system. For some reason, looking back on it now, I realize coaches absolutely knew that I didn't run a 4.59. This was likely one of the many reasons I didn't receive the offers I envisioned.

- Avoid any pictures, ensure you are using proper grammar, and keep the email brief. College coaches receive hundreds of emails a day. If you have a brick of text without any important information, it will be moved to the trash pile. If you are fortunate enough to have a coach take the time to open your email, don't screw up that opportunity by authoring a short biography including the name of your dog in the body of the email.

Try to contact the Recruiting Coordinator/Position Coach/Head Coach of the schools you are reaching out to. Take the time to personalize every email with the coach's name and suit it toward them. This is a part of the process where it is necessary to be relentless—you can email coaches every week over and over if they do not respond. No response is not a "We are not interested." They may have not opened your email, they may have meant to email you back and forgot. Whatever the case may be, if you have not received a "no," then the option of being recruited by that school is still on the table. You will want to target hundreds of coaches at a minimum. Every email is an opportunity, and you can never have too many open doors. The story of Monte Gaddis is an example of persisting until you get an answer. The former Towson University linebacker stood outside the Cleveland Browns' facility for three days with a cardboard sign written on it: "Will do ALL drills! Starving for my 1st shot. WHY NOT?" Eventually he got a chance to speak with the General Manager and Monte delivered his game film directly to the General Manager. This is an example of not taking no for an answer. If you want to create an opportunity for yourself, the first step is right in front of you. Every email you send and every camp you attend you are separating yourself from the thousands of players skipping that step in the process.

Your game tape is the single biggest piece in the recruiting process. When it comes to creating your highlight tape it is extremely important to make sure you are showcasing your absolute best football ability. It is not necessary to have a professional do this or to pay a service. Follow the next steps, and feel free contact me if you would like feedback on your highlight tape. Players should be developing film from as early as their first plays on Varsity. As a freshman or junior varsity player you should not be focusing on recruiting, simply work on developing your game and excelling in the classroom. We discussed the fact that college coaches' time is very valuable, and they will not watch an entire highlight tape unless the first one to three plays catch their attention as a potential fit. Typically, the video will be closed within the first fifteen seconds. I have seen this first hand as a player watching my coaches open emails of prospective players. It is a vicious process. Here are some things to consider when piecing together your highlight tape:

- Am I showcasing my best technique?

- Am I displaying hustle and relentlessness?

- Does this film separate myself from other players?

- Am I displaying versatility on the field?

- How is the competition level of my opponent?

Let's visualize a concrete example. A defensive back's highlight tape may consist of a variety of interceptions, pass breakups, run stops, open field tackles, and special teams plays. One common mistake is that athletes tend to put all of their interceptions or touchdowns at the beginning of the highlight tape simply because they are "big plays" and a flashy statistic. If you are playing cover four and the quarterback overthrows a pass directly toward you, it is not deserving of the first play on your highlight. College coaches aren't looking for plays that any player could make. They are looking for exceptional plays. A tight, quick break on a receiver's route and a pass breakup showcases a lot more transferrable skills than a tipped interception off of a receiver's hands will. Genuinely evaluate your competition and your own performance as if you were a coach. This is a part of the process where it pays off to be humble and dissect your own skills. What are you showcasing? You want to direct your best plays to the beginning of your highlight and ideally demonstrate the ability to be a versatile football player. As a lineman it is extremely important to consider the quality of your opponent; a great pass rush that doesn't result in a sack is a better showcase than a bullrush on a 165-pound left tackle. You want to show what is most closely translated to the next level. Here are a few position-specific qualities to showcase:

Quarterback: Decision Making (You may have thrown a touchdown, but if it was in double coverage it does not display strong decision-making ability). Arm Strength, Accuracy, Mobility, Pocket Presence.

Running Back: Speed (acceleration through holes, separation from defenders), Vision (reading blocks and making the correct cuts), Toughness (falling forward, initiating contact, breaking tackles), Elusiveness (making defenders miss), Pass Blocking (stepping up, versatility).

Wide Receiver: Releases (technique), Footwork (precise breaks, efficient use of hands and feet), Route Running (attacking leverage, spatial awareness), Hands (catching in traffic, high pointing the ball, attacking the ball), Yards after catch.

Tight End: Similar to WR with addition of ability to pass block and run block.

Offensive Lineman: First step (pass set, as well as run drive), Effort (are you looking for work constantly?), Aggression (are you attacking the defense?), Strength (physical size and ability to move defenders), Technique (hand placement, leverage, pulling/slide protection).

Defensive Lineman: First step (are the other defensive lineman getting out quicker than you?), Technique (variety of speed/power moves), Strength (ability to fight through blocks, get penetration), Finish (wrapping up QB, stopping progress of RB on tackles).

Linebacker: Football IQ (are you hitting the hole? Taking correct angles on blitzes/pass drops?), Tackling (ball carrier failing to gain any yards after contact, forcing turnovers), Versatility (can you display zone and man pass defense? Fill holes? Blitz off the edge?), Pursuit (how close are you to the football each play?).

Defensive Back: Agility (how quick can you stop and start? Do you recover from a misstep? Are your hips smooth while changing direction?), Vision (do you see the field in zone? Are you breaking on routes?),

Coverage (are you able to guard a wide receiver in off-man and press technique?)

At the end of the day coaches want to see what you're capable of on the field. If potential won games on Saturdays, coaches would recruit differently. Coaches recruit on what they feel they are guaranteed to bring into their program. Being recruited off potential would end up costing college football programs thousands of dollars in the long run.

C. Communication

There will be a few main points of contact between athletes and coaches as an opportunity to get exposure: contacting coaches via email, contacting coaches via social media, attending combines, and attending in-person prospect camps on campuses. Attending recruiting camps is by far and away the most successful and effective method of gaining exposure.

We've already briefly touched on the process of emailing. It is undoubtedly a grind– I probably received in between ten and twelve responses for every 300 emails I sent out during my high school and junior college recruitment. Of those responses, a handful may have turned into phone calls and actual conversations that developed into recruitment. Do not let a low response rate discourage you, it is simply a numbers game. Chances are a vast majority of the coaches may not have even opened your email. Some schools aren't looking for certain positions, or they don't recruit certain states, and they likely won't take the time to watch or respond to a message if this is the case. Be persistent, keep pushing, and knock them out. The intent should always be to get noticed by one more school each day. There is no valid reason you should not be able to send a hundred emails in a couple hours. Do not send emails during the season on a Friday, Saturday, or Sunday. Think like a football player. Coaches realistically are not taking the time to watch highlight videos during these times. Coaches are traveling, playing, celebrating, and preparing during the weekends. The best times to contact coaches in-season are mornings in the early week. Included here are a few sample email titles and a template to use. I wouldn't recommend copying the template word for word, rather you should use it as a broad approach to expand on and alter.

High school Subject: 6'2" WR Class of 2020 Highlights (3.4 GPA/25 ACT)- Athlete Name

JUCO Subject: 6'2" WR December Grad 2/2 (3.5 GPA)- Athlete Name

In your subject, you want to highlight one of your qualities that separates you immediately. Whether it is a physical measurable, academic success, recruiting interest, accolades, etc. A generic title such as "2020 WR Highlights- Name" won't catch anyone's attention.

Sample Body:

Hello Coach (Coach Name),

My name is (Athlete Name). I am a (Height, Weight, Position) in the class of (20XX). In my career I have accomplished (brief list of awards/statistics–don't overdo it). I am interested in (School Name) and your football program. I am also currently being recruited by (List Schools). I feel like I would be a great fit in your program. I can be reached at (Phone Number) or you can contact my head coach (Coach's Name) at (Coach's Phone Number/Email).

Thanks,

(Athlete Contact Info, School, Class, Position)

I realize how simple and straight forward this email appears. However, for many student athletes it may be their first experience with recruitment or reaching out to coaches. It doesn't have to be a reinvention of the wheel–your film will speak for itself. The biggest takeaway is to not write anything in an email that would make a coach not want to recruit you: overconfidence, poor grammar, lack of attention to detail, etc. Ensure you have no spelling mistakes and that you are entering the proper school name and coach name every email. Remember to reach out to your coach to confirm they are okay with you including their contact information. You should also forward your highlights, test scores and GPA, and vitals to your head coach with a list of schools you are interested in. Let your coach know which schools you are targeting and ask him to send an email to the coach if he feels it is an appropriate fit. Do not feel offended if your coach doesn't email certain schools. This is the reality of coaches selling their players–they will ultimately only sell you as strongly as they feel comfortable. My defensive back coach during junior college used to joke around about this saying "If I sell you to a school, you better not make me look stupid. Because that will be the last time I get to talk to that coach and you're screwing it up for everyone else." Harsh, but a true reality in the recruiting world.

Social media can be a great asset in addition to emails during the recruiting process. In this day and age coaches are very active on social media, constantly branding and representing their program. Follow coaches, post your highlight, direct message them, etc. This is very similar to email aside from the very important fact you have to be sure your social media page represents who you are as a person. Be extremely careful what you retweet, like, post, and engage in on social media. Coaches have pulled scholarships from recruits solely based on their activity on social media. Northwestern Head Coach Pat Fitzgerald shared his thoughts on the subject while speaking at the Positive Coaching Alliance. Touching base on his position coaches investigating recruits' red flags on social media pages he stated:

"I want to know what the deal is, and until you can give me that answer, we're not going to progress. And that eliminates a lot of issues on the front. I would rather have a one-day problem than a four-year problem."

One tweet can be the difference between a Division I program recruiting you, and removing you from their list. You have head coaches at the highest level of college football making these statements, and many more on Twitter every day. Your social media page is a digital blueprint of the type of person you are. Do not create a separate account for recruitment as an alternative, thinking you can just goof off and be inappropriate on a second account. This is an obvious attempt to hide something on your regular account. A high-character person won't have to change anything about their social media or persona when going through the recruiting process. This isn't to say when I was going through recruiting I didn't go back and delete a ton of content on my pages. The reality is, many athletes are teenagers who are developing their personal identity, going through a maturation process, and most likely have posted or endorsed something online they may not currently agree with. It may not be a bad idea to go through your old posts and clear out some of the content that could be considered questionable. You might even find some cheap laughs, maybe confessing your love for a modern hip-hop artist or posting "To be honest, you're cute and we should hang out sometime!" on your crush's Facebook page. Thirteen-year-old you and eighteen-year-old you are hopefully different people. Not only is this a smart idea for recruitment, but as well as potential job searches in the future. Coaches are looking at what type of person you are just as much as your athletic ability. It is a poor business investment for a coach to invest in you as an athlete if you can't stay eligible and on campus. All the talent and athletic ability in the world will serve no use from a living room couch. Out of all the potential reasons athletes don't get the chance to play at the next level, social media is the easiest one to manage. Don't be that guy.

College camps are truly the best opportunity to get offers in high school and connect with coaches. My alma matter Concordia-St Paul, hosted the Twin Cities showcase with over thirty college coaches in attendance this past summer. Coaches were able to watch a padded practice. Players received several scholarship offers on the spot from multiple schools. Many times, a coach does not need to see your film if they can evaluate you in person. Stay away from camps you have to pay to attend, especially if there are no college coaches in attendance. Third parties claim to do combine testing, as well as sending your information out to schools. This is a waste of money and time. Get to campuses where you can visit a school, see the area, and meet the coaches yourself. I attended two in high school that were great experiences. I picked schools within driving distance that were affordable trips for my family to make happen. Your high school coach should encourage you to attend camps in the summer. Go out of your way to introduce yourself to coaches, give them your contact information, and make connections. But as we've said before, your first priority should be competing. Coaches will approach you if you are dominating on the field. Camps are the number one way to get exposure for recruits, period! There are only a few elite reputable combines that are worth attending. These are opportunities for high level recruits to compete against the best of the best. Do not pay $100 to go to a local field and go through a gauntlet of meaningless drills you could do for free. Save yourself the time and effort. The money and time spent traveling to local combines is better spent on the road in the summer. I attended a combine in high school that was $100. We ran our forty-yard-dash (on an unofficial timer), did two reps of one on ones, and did a couple position drills. There was no film taken, and no college coaches in attendance, making the day a complete waste of time and money. The combine claimed to send your vitals and results from testing to hundreds of colleges. Without your game film, this is essentially a scam. Be wary of what services you are paying for exactly. Some of these services have no problem preying on opportunistic athletes and stealing their money.

Now that you have developed your highlight film, contacted, and spoken to coaches, it is time to start separating schools that are seriously recruiting you and moving toward deciding on a school. To be blunt, if you are finished with your senior season of sport and you don't have a Division I offer, or any official visits lined up, it is time to put that vision to rest for the time being. Start focusing on the hundreds of other programs still in the middle of their recruitment. The majority of Division I schools are offering scholarships to athletes their sophomore and junior season, occasionally during their senior season at the latest. Do not listen to your parents if they are pumping your head full of delusional ideas. You absolutely have to be realistic with yourself and figure out which schools want you to come play for them. This is a part of the process where many athletes and families completely miss the point. Any schools showing interest in you is an opportunity to continue playing your sport, possibly for a significant financial discount, all while pursuing your degree. Having the mindset of "Division I or bust" is detrimental to athletes who don't fit that mold. There are tons of great academic and athletic programs at every division. Determining serious interest is not a complicated process. Coaches who are seriously recruiting you will contact you via phone call, offer in-person visits (depending on proximity), and will be discussing monetary value of scholarship offers and scheduling official visits.

I had received letters from Tulane, New Mexico State, and Northern Arizona University in high school. None of these schools could probably even tell you what state I lived in or what position I played. I was one of thousands of kids receiving the letters, and I knew it. I didn't ever take them seriously. This is a difficult concept for a lot of kids to grasp, only because they don't know better. How could you blame them? I'm sure these letters generate interest and excitement in the parents even more than the athletes in some scenarios. In my high school yearbook one of my teammates was quoted saying he had a Division I football offer that he was "deciding" if he wanted to take. This player didn't play our senior year due to injury and had only received a generic letter that every kid in the state of Arizona got. These were automated letters sent out based on recruiting questionnaires. Letters, marketing emails, and the occasional texts are indicators a school has you on their radar as a possible backup or walk-on target and will likely not offer you.

I had a coach text me during my recruitment, "Hey Andrew! Does the Salt Lake freeze in December?" It was a good sign of interest from a coach, besides the fact I lived in Arizona and had never seen Salt Lake. This was a sign to me that the coach probably wasn't recruiting me too seriously. Coaches will often keep sporadic communication, but this doesn't necessarily always reflect their interest level. Don't be afraid to tell coaches where you stand with your financial situation, expectations, and your value. At the same time you want to be careful not to burn any bridges. Never turn down a school or stop responding to them because you feel you are too big time for them. This will only result in negative attention. Any coach that is showing interest in you is an amazing opportunity that should be treated with gratitude. Even if the school is not an appropriate fit, be sure to tell the coach with the bare minimum of a text showing your gratitude for their interest. I personally called up all the schools' coaches that recruited me once I committed to another school, taking the time to thank them for recruiting me and letting them know I had made my decision in my best interest. I believe most coaches appreciate being forthright and full honesty through the process. I had attempted to get a teammate of mine from junior college recruited to Concordia-St. Paul. Our head coach offered him a scholarship, took the time, and went to eat dinner with his family at his home, and the athlete eventually just stopped responding to our coaching staff, eventually committing to an in-conference opponent. This is unfortunately common behavior amongst recruits, and it enforces bad habits. Nobody enjoys the feeling of being disregarded– after every failed job interview I've attended, it always felt slightly better if I received an email letting me know I hadn't gotten the position. As your recruiting process comes to an end reflect on your experience, celebrate your achievements, and make the decision with the feeling of relief and pride that you earned.

Things to consider when you make the big decision:

- Schools Academic Profile (Do they have your major? If you are undecided, how do they rank nationally? What are the class sizes?)

- Campus Life (Is the enrollment smaller than your high school? Is the city or town one you can see yourself enjoying for four or five years? Are you satisfied with the living arrangements and facilities of the school?)

- Location (Will your family and friends ever get to see you play? Is there snow on the ground five months a year? Is the town's greatest attraction Buffalo Wild Wings?) I had a coach recruiting me during high school explain to me that a group of guys on their team would carpool on Fridays to drive 45 minutes to go to Buffalo Wild Wings. I lived 20 minutes outside of Phoenix. Needless to say, the meeting with the coach did not have me eager to pick up a pen and sign my move to Kansas.

- Financial Package (Do you have to take out student loans? How much? What is the cost of living for off-campus housing in the area?). I was offered a full-tuition scholarship to an NAIA university in a major metropolitan city. The cost of living would be approximately $14,000 a year to stay in the student housing. I had an offer from a different school that was half-tuition, where I would be paying significantly less in total based on cost of living and tuition rate. The dollar sign on the scholarship is not the only factor to consider. You can be eating steak in Nebraska and ramen noodles in Chicago with similar scholarship offers.

- Coaches/Culture (Have the coaches shown a desire to have you in their program? Do you relate to the coaches? Are the coaches able to bring out the best in you as an athlete and a person? Were you welcomed by current players on a visit or at camp?)

- Football Program (Will you play as a freshman or redshirt? Is the school competing for conference championships? Do they play a similar scheme to what you played in high school?)

There will be several voices giving you advice and their opinions on which school to pick. Having been through the recruiting process twice, I know that no matter what, you will feel like someone will be disappointed in your decision. Always put yourself first, as ultimately this decision is going to impact the rest of your life. If people in your circle aren't showing anything less than proud support, they should not be in your circle. The simplest, most accurate advice I received was, "You go wherever the shoe fits." Your foot is the only foot shaped like it– every person has different interests and preferences. The school that is the best fit for you may very well not be the school your mother, best friend, girlfriend or boyfriend, or high school coach wanted you to pick. You earned the right to make your decision, you put in the work, you endured the emotions and stress of the recruiting process. Take the time to enjoy signing and picking a school.

I knew I was going to commit to Concordia-St. Paul while I was on my official visit. I was staying at the Radisson Hotel in Roseville. I loved everything about St. Paul when I visited. I got off the plane in April from Arizona wearing shorts and a t-shirt, only to be greeted with snow flurries. My final night as I looked out the window of my hotel, I experienced complete emotional achievement. The feeling was indescribable. Tears of joy for a moment, and then the weight of the world off my shoulders. Everything I sacrificed was for something. The anxiety and undeniable fear of failure that I had carried for three years was gone. I had worked for that moment for years, lost friends, skipped out on tons of parties, trips, and experiences. I worked 25 hours a week washing dishes during my senior season of football in high school. I did two-a-days the entire summer going into my senior season. I paid my trainer out of pocket to train in the mornings before 7-on-7 and weights in the evening. I jammed rocks in the door of my junior college weight room to be able to workout at 1 AM. I slept in my car in the parking lot when I commuted to school when I was tired. I cried tears of frustration many times during junior college behind closed doors. People didn't understand, people criticized, people hated, some people even laughed at me. It didn't matter. I got what I had strived for. It was mine. My goal is for you to experience this feeling, as you will carry it for the rest of your life in everything that you do. This is just the first step in a long journey— a commitment without the action to follow through is meaningless.

To offer some input from a coach's perspective, I asked my former coach Trevor Warner to give his take on recruiting for athletes. Coach Warner is a former All-American performer at the Division III level, and he has coached Division IA, II, and currently III. Here is what he had to say:

RECRUITING ADVICE 101
FROM A COLLEGE FOOTBALL COACH

I want to start out by saying I have played at the Division III level and coached at the Division IA, II, and III levels. I am what would be known as a *young* coach. I understand what many kids today are going through and thinking. Not too long ago, I was in your shoes trying to find my next home. I don't claim to know everything about recruiting, but I do know a few things. Here are some key tips I believe are important for athletes to understand when going through the recruiting process.

1. Recruiting is like dating.

You heard that right. Coaches are looking for a certain type of kid. Not just athletically, but more importantly, a fit for the program's culture. They want to know if you'll be a good fit for the team. If you're not athletically able to play at that level, they won't be interested in you being a part of their program. They get hired and fired solely based on performance. Like dating, finding the right fit for the student-athlete only works if there is mutual interest. If you're wanted by a Division II school, but all you want is to be at a Division I school, you may run into some issues. Understand who is showing interest in you and go where you're wanted. Understanding this will make the recruiting process much easier to handle.

2. Coaches want more "Big Fish in a Little Pond" type guys.

Coaches' philosophies at all levels are to find the kids that will be some of the best in the entire country. For instance, coaches at the Division III level want to get as many kids that have Division II talent on their roster as possible. That's the same for Division II and Division IA. If you have interest from multiple Division IA schools your junior year, but never get offered by those programs, they're showing you that they don't *really* want you. If you have 5+ Division II offers, but those Division IAA schools keep calling and texting without taking the recruiting process to the next step, it might be because they're just keeping you "warm."

3. Coaches must keep you "warm," so you don't lose interest in their program.

Maybe a coach has called you once or twice, exchanged a few texts over the year, and seems pretty interested in you. He hasn't offered to get you on campus, made a home-visit or campus-visit, and he hasn't offered you a scholarship. But you get excited when he contacts you. He is, what we as coaches say, "keeping you warm." He is maintaining your interest in their program so when the other kids they really want go elsewhere, he can come in and offer you last minute if necessary.

4. Ask the tough questions at the appropriate times.

Every staff has a process of recruiting, and collectively they must be on the same page to be effective and efficient. There must be a large amount of communication and understanding of what is wanted from each position coach. If you play quarterback and the defensive line coach contacts you, it's most likely because you're a part of his geographical area. If he shows interest and says he will send your film over to the quarterback coach and offensive coordinator, follow up with him. If you don't hear back from him in a week, ask him what the other coaches thought of your film. There are a few questions that I would advise all student athletes to ask coaches. Some differ based on level of play and if the division allows scholarships to be offered or not. First, if talking to a Division IA or Division II coach, I would ask how they break up their scholarships. I would ask them what a typical athletic scholarship looks like for an incoming freshman. I would also ask them what the average amount of total aid kids on their roster have. Some Division II programs don't have the maximum number of scholarships the NCAA allows (36). I would ask them how many they have and what portion of the team are "walk-ons." Second, no matter who you're talking to, I would ask where you stand on their recruiting board for your position. All coaches have an evaluation process and ranking system to be as precise as possible when recruiting. If you ask them tough questions, you force them to be honest and peel back a few layers. Some can lie when answering, but most won't feel comfortable lying to a 16-year-old kid.

5. Separate yourself in the way you contact coaches.

We understand that student-athletes are tech savvy. We also understand they're addicted to their phones. We get hundreds of emails and Twitter messages every week from recruits. Efficiency is important for us. When emailing us, include an introduction that explains you. We will see what type of player you are when we watch your film. We want to know who you are. Include your test scores and grade point average. Include your physical information (Height, Weight, Lifting personal records, Forty-yard-dash time,

Pro-agility time). Include your film link. Double check your message for any spelling or grammatical errors. Essentially, make it as easy as possible for us to find out as much as possible in the shortest amount of time. The biggest way to separate yourself in my opinion is to include the coaches' name(s), along with the school name and either the mascot or something about the school. This shows us you took the time to write the message out and you didn't just copy and paste. Show interest if you want to get interest.

Another unique way to display interest in a program is to write letters. I understand many of you probably have never done this. It takes time. It takes effort. It's harder than typing a message on your iPhone. But it will immediately gain the attention of the coaches and show them you're interested. Even if they decide you're not the right fit for their program, your letter still was read. That doesn't always happen with email and social media.

6. If a coach asks you to apply and submit transcripts or test scores, do it as quickly as possible.

If you're interested in a program, show them you're interested by applying and submitting all academic information needed to admissions shortly after they advise you to do so. If a coach asks you to apply, and then a month goes by and you still haven't, you've indicated that you either can't follow directions or you blatantly don't value time. Coaches at any level don't like either of those things. Get stuff done quickly and show you can be counted on, even to the littlest details.

7. Don't play games with coaches.

Best thing you can do is be honest and open with the coaches. Try not to confuse coaches to thinking one thing, and then pull a fast one on them. Be honest. Be open. Be clear about what you want and what you're looking for. If they can provide it, they'll tell you they can or can't. If you want to study chemistry and they only have biology, be clear with them about what you want. Like dating, when the coaches or student-athletes play games, it makes the whole process harder.

8. Have a wholistic view of what school you want.

When looking for a school and going through this process, talk with your parents and friends early on about what you want. For me, I wanted to attend a school that I would get a great degree from and be set up for success in my career. I wanted to be an impact player on the field and be a big fish in a small pond, compared to a small fish in a big pond. I wanted to be a part of a community that was tight, that forced me to think differently and grow in the way I saw the world. Ultimately, I was looking for a small school that had good football where I could play early on and get a great academic experience. Some people don't want that, and that's fine, but if you know what you want prior to talking with coaches, you can ask questions you may have that they can inform you about those areas of interest.

At the end of the day, the recruiting process can be stressful and daunting at times. Finding the right college is likely the first major decision you are faced with making in your young life. We hope you take this advice and hope it aids you throughout this process and sets you up for success.

Coach Warner provides insight I am unable to offer having never been a coach, take it with value.

RECRUITING QUICK TIPS:

- Focus on being the best player in the country before you focus on being the most recruited player.

- Be extremely careful of the image you present to coaches and the community on your social media pages. Coaches are looking for high-character athletes.

- Avoid paying a recruiting service or social media guru to put together a highlight tape or assist with your recruiting. Everything can be done by yourself for free just as effectively. Save that money to invest in traveling to camps during the summer.

- Trust in the process and do not get discouraged by your interest as the months go on. If you want to play at the next level you will need to do everything in your power to have a fighting chance. You only need one coach to take a shot and invest in you for your dream to become a reality.

3
ACADEMICS

WHY WASTE A free college education? Why waste your athletic talents by being ineligible? Why work so hard toward your goals, but neglect the most important piece?

These are the questions I unfortunately found myself asking during high school and college. Too many times I witnessed my teammates throw away and take for granted the game of football, the game that provides an opportunity for many to pursue a brighter future. Academics were never a point of struggle for me because I invested as much time toward school as I did football. I have my parents to thanks for this. I realize this is not the reality for every, or even a majority of athletes in high school and college. The fact of the matter is great athletes' habits translate directly to the classroom. Notice the language there, great athletes' habits, not their talent, translate directly to the classroom. Lifting weights is the equivalent of doing your homework. Practicing is showing up to class. Watching game film is studying. Winning on Saturdays is performing well on tests and exams. During high school, if you are struggling with your coursework you need to approach your teacher and get extra assistance. I had an open period during my senior year of high school that allowed me a late start. I eventually used this extra time to sit in my math teacher's class and work on my classwork. Now truthfully, this was part of a contract I signed to remain eligible. I was failing AP Calculus, however my teacher allowed me to participate as long as I abided by our contract. This taught me a valuable lesson, though: had I initially been going in during the year for help when I needed it, I most likely wouldn't have gotten to the point where I was failing. It is okay to admit when you are struggling in a class. Be honest with your coaches and teachers; however, just know if you are not submitting your work, or showing up on time and paying attention, teacher's will quickly dismiss your call for help. The two important points relating to athletics and academics are understanding the requirements to qualify and remain eligible, as well as developing habits that translate to success in the classroom. First let's discuss the initial part of the equation: what exactly is required of you as a student athlete at the high-school level to qualify for NCAA eligibility.

The bare minimum requirements to play at the NCAA level include:

- Taking 16 core courses:
- Four years of English
- Three years of math (Algebra 1 or higher)

- Two years of natural/physical science (including one year of lab science if your high school offers it)

- One additional year of English, math, or natural/physical science

- Two years of social science

- Four additional years of English, math, natural/physical science, social science, foreign language, comparative religion or philosophy

These core classes require a minimum GPA of 2.0. This information is easily accessible via Google and can be accessed on the NCAA website. I wanted to introduce the concept of academic eligibility to stress the importance and effects it will have later in your college career. Challenge yourself as much as possible in the classroom; the benefits are not only financial, but will also save you time. Acquiring a few AP credits can be the difference between taking four or five courses in your spring semester during college. If you aren't aware, that is a handful of hours a week for an entire semester and a few thousand dollars in most cases. The alternative would be taking nineteen credits a semester for several years to graduate on time, like I did. I would not recommend this, and had I any other choice I would have avoided that type of course load being an athlete.

Succeeding academically in high school can earn you thousands of dollars in scholarships, give you more availability for schools to recruit you, and set yourself up for continued success in college and the workforce by becoming a strong student. If you scrape by with that 2.1 GPA in high school and happen to qualify for the NCAA, good luck remaining eligible during college when you have countless more responsibilities and stressors with a harder workload. It is not a coincidence that some of the strongest academic schools in the country carry a reputation of phenomenal football programs as well. When the demand and expectation for excellence is held high in the classroom, that demand is carried into athletics.

The big tests to prepare for are your college entrance exams known as the ACT and SAT. Your GPA is important, but these exam scores are the national standard for college entrance and every college coach will ask you what your score is before they recruit you. When it comes to college applications, schools will look more heavily at your test scores in comparison to your GPA. If you can afford a paid tutor that is a great approach to preparing for these exams. There are several effective reputable services that offer in-person, and online coaching specifically for the ACT and SAT. The money paid for a tutor service can easily pay itself back in scholarship money if you are able to improve your score. I did not prepare in any manner for my exams, and there is no doubt in my mind I could have scored higher had I taken the time to at least engage in some free prep materials. Set aside an hour every Saturday and Sunday throughout your junior year to prepare for the exams. If you did this beginning in football season that would accumulate to approximately 60 extra hours of preparation. It may seem like a small number, but cramming all day the day before the exam would account for eight hours, most of which you wouldn't retain.

The SAT and ACT each contain 4 parts– it is recommended to focus on each section for a couple weeks at a time, while implementing review sessions to refer to the sections you aren't currently studying. This is a habit that translates directly to studying for any midterm or final exam in college. Attempting to memorize the entire semester's material during the last week of the semester is a sure-fire way to struggle on your final exams. Instead, the approach should be every single weekend throughout the year to review what you covered in the previous week before beginning the next week's course load. With this habit, you are covering every week's material several times. The information then becomes knowledge rather than a memorized statistic. The techniques practiced in college entrance exams will hopefully become second-nature. You should be able to see a question, identify the method you need to demonstrate to answer it, and execute effectively. Reading a question and immediately realizing you've seen the material but don't understand how to do it is one of the most frustrating experiences as a student. This typically happens when you try to "cram" and study for an exam last minute. Your brain can recall seeing the question, but it doesn't remember how to solve the problem. This is because it has only had one repetition. Now for an athletic analogy, I want you to go shoot fifteen three-pointers and count how many you make. Practice one hour for six weeks and try again. I'm sure you will hit a higher percentage of your shots attempted. It seems extremely simple in terms of shooting a basketball, but it is the same exact principle applied to studying for an exam.

You can take the exams multiple times while only sending your best scores to colleges. The recommended time to take the exams is during the spring of junior year. There are several free resources online that can be retrieved by a simple google search of "Free ACT/SAT prep." With the amount of resources available online today there is no excuse to say you weren't given the tools to prepare. It is simply a matter of going to the school library and putting in some extra hours studying. In some instances, one point on the ACT could realistically be a $2000-4000 gain or loss in terms of academic scholarship money. Go to any college's website and click on the tuition and rates page. You will find a link for scholarships, and there will be a sliding scale for money awarded as a freshman based on your test scores and GPA. As an example, if you utilize the Arizona State University incoming freshman scholarship calculator, you will see two students with the same exact GPA and a 1-point difference in their test scores will have a $1000 differential in their scholarships.

It is important to realize, there is undoubtedly a player in the country with the same exact physical measurables and production as yourself. The guy with the better grades will get the opportunity. At all levels of football below Division I, partial scholarships are the norm. If you have similar talent as another player, but you received more academic money, the coaches are more likely to offer you because it may potentially cost them less money from their school's football scholarship fund. It is a numbers game. The emphasis of academics cannot be stressed enough to any student athlete aspiring to compete in college.

As a student-athlete you should be as ambitious in the classroom as you are on the field. If you are able to take AP classes, go for it. If you are interested in joining academic clubs or pursuing extra-curricular educational opportunities, do it. Football will end for everyone at some point. Your education is the backbone of your professional career moving forward. In high school your priorities are maintaining a high GPA and scoring as high as possible on your college entrance exams. Taking a step back to the concept of intent, it is important to realize what your intent is as a student. Is your intent to get a 3.5 GPA? This is a measurable, and respectable goal for any student in the country, and most people would say this is a successful mark for any student to shoot for. The other perspective would be, for example, having the intent to learn how to manage a budget and payroll for a business you plan to start after college. The idea here is, both intents would hopefully result in high GPAs and successful classes. The difference being, one intent is to prepare for the future by gaining knowledge and workplace skills. The other student is simply aiming for a number on the transcript. You can certainly get a 3.5 GPA by skating by and cramming last minute to pass your classes. The student who is in the library every week and is excited about their education and future may also finish with that 3.5 GPA. You don't have to guess which student will likely secure the better job after graduation. The intent of your academic experience will be all the difference as you move from high school to college.

In college there are several aspects of your education that are different from high school. Your window of opportunity to make poor decisions gets larger, not smaller. You will have less structure in your academic schedule, and no one will force you to go to class or wake up on time. Generally your day will consist of two or three classes each day, or in some scenarios three or four classes one day and one the other. Class periods are longer and the curriculum will be more advanced from high school. You will be challenged from the new material and given less individual instruction. Even on small campuses you may find it difficult to make connections with professors in some cases. Ultimately in college you will get treated like an adult, meaning all the resources are available for you to use, but the initiative lies on you. No one will hold your hand and escort you to the tutoring office or class. If you do make the decision to skip class, expect to find coaches walking around campus poking their heads in classes to check on you. On our campus, a single missed class would earn you a "towel-push". This workout occurred at 5:30 AM in the gymnasium. I couldn't tell you my experience with it because I never endured one, however I only heard awful reviews.

The football program will certainly have a mandatory study hall (whether you have a 4.0 or a 2.0 GPA, first-year players as transfers/freshman are required to attend). This is another wrench in your schedule in which consequences will apply if you miss. There is no excuse to not pass your classes and succeed in college. You have academic tutoring centers, mandatory study hall, and plenty of time if you set your priorities straight. Clubs and academic groups are excellent opportunities to network and build connections outside of your football program. I graduated college with few academic connections, as I did not challenge myself to step outside of the football culture and branch out to other groups on campus. This ultimately hurt me in the long run, and I struggled with finding an initial job opportunity after college. After I graduated, I found myself standing around looking to my left and right, searching for an internship with no real connections or peers to contact. I had a Summa Cum Laude Degree, and athletics as the backbone of my resume. This likely won't get your foot in the door at your first choice after graduation in the current job market. Clubs, extra-curriculars, and professors are amazing resources if you build strong relationships throughout college. Don't look at academics as a requirement to compete in sports, but rather an investment in your future. If you put money in a stock, you are investing in it, hoping for it to earn dividends on return and make your money back and more. Tuition is a fee, and whether it is covered by scholarship or not, it should be viewed as an investment in your education and personal development, which increases your potential earnings after graduation (your dividends).

There are undeniable benefits of graduating with your degree as a student-athlete. In every job interview

I participated in after graduation I was able to pull answers from my experience as a student athlete and display it as a strong quality. Student athletes are more likely to report having professors that cared about them as a person in comparison to non-student athletes. Engagement in the classroom and with professors is an indicator of well-being in the years following college. There are plenty of reasons and evidence as to why everyone should value their education; athletes fortunate enough to be receiving an education for free or at a discounted price should see these reasons as clear as day.

ACADEMICS QUICK TIPS:

- Don't look at study hall as an annoying requirement. Be grateful you have dedicated time set aside each week to focus on your schoolwork without distraction.

- Sit in the front of the class and show up on time. You should have zero absences unless you are traveling or sick. In these scenarios, connect with your professor several weeks in advance to confirm what the lesson plan is for the class period.

- Do not wear your headphones, text, or put your head on your desk inside the classroom. This is not only disrespectful to the professor speaking, it also says as a student you don't value your education. This makes it difficult to ask professors for favors or assistance when needed.

- Join a club or organization on campus, connect with students outside of the football program that share your professional or academic interests.

- Become familiar with the computer labs, study rooms, and library hours on campus. You will inevitably have to print something last minute at one point or another and you will want to know when the library is open. I walked to campus through the snow several times, only to find the library closed. Don't make that easily avoidable mistake.

- Set reminders in your phone for when important projects and tests are due.

- Dedicate a certain amount of time each week to work independently in the library. The atmosphere rejects any distractions and allows you to have all your resources right within reach.

- If you are undecided on a major, select courses that are broader and apply to several different areas. Don't select Criminal Justice as a humanity if you know you won't be in that field, unless you are genuinely interested in the material. Don't chase "Easy A's." Challenge yourself.

- Have a written weekly schedule. You may have a research paper that isn't due for two months, but you should have written on your schedule "Work on Research Paper" every week.

The end goal is to hold that degree in your hand at the end of the four or five years you are in school. Following the advice in this chapter will prepare you for developing the critical habits that will make academics feel much easier, allowing you to learn and grow as much as possible during college.

4
CAMPUS LIFE

I COULD NEVER forget the team meeting Sunday morning following my first college game. I was a seventeen-year-old freshman and still lived at home commuting to my junior college– everything about college was brand new at the time. We lost on the road after missing a short game-winning field goal as time expired. Our coach came in the room, and saw players with their heads down and wearing sunglasses inside of the dark classroom. He opened by saying someone looked like they were at the club last night and shook his head as he let out a sigh. There was an awkward silence followed by a pause in which coach cracked a smile and said "I know what's up, guys. The first thing I learned in college was… win or lose, you still booze." The entire team broke into laughter. After settling down, we got to business preparing for our next opponent. Our coach didn't spend much time at all focusing on the loss. It was a catchy expression, but it is often the reality of college campuses nationwide. I didn't go out after that loss, and neither did many of my teammates. There were always groups of guys discussing the after-party plans on the bus ride regardless of the outcome of the game. This is just the nature of college culture, and athletes are not an exception. The most recent NCAA goals study completed in June of 2018 found that 77% of NCAA athletes reported drinking alcohol in the last year. More than half of the student athletes that admitted drinking were also guilty of binge drinking. While college students and student athletes are still maturing and finding their identities, experimenting with new experiences and social groups is common. The unfortunate and sad reality is many athletes every year ruin their athletic careers due to their poor choices within campus life. It is easy to get caught up with the distractions of the environment and ultimately lose sight of why you pursued college in the first place.

On a summer night during my junior year, I had come home from a long night of work and my roommates were planning to throw a party. Typically, I would have participated and been a good host, however I was worn out from work this night and headed upstairs to my room, going to bed early. I woke up a few hours later to three women running into my room screaming. They shut the door behind them and turned on the light. I rolled over in my underwear and rubbed my eyes, not quite sure if this was a dream or not. After I came to my senses, I realized there was complete chaos downstairs and I could hear screaming and people running throughout the house. The girls told me someone pulled a gun out during the party. Awesome. I slipped on my Air Force One's and some sweat shorts and went to find my roommates. I didn't recognize anyone in the house, and it was completely dark downstairs with some groups of people still standing around as I turned the corner of the staircase. Apparently, some kid pulled a "fake gun" out and eventually ran across the street during the drama. We shut down the party and the cops were called, who eventually helped us clear it out. They were cool enough to give us that option to avoid giving us a ticket. Luckily no one was injured, and the kid never came back. The lesson being, plenty of times you are going to be at a party or bar in an environment where there are people you don't know. You must be careful of your surroundings and always be conscious about your decision making, especially as a student athlete. Several times during college I was woken during my sleep to some drama at a party in my house, it was always hilarious to see drunk partiers reactions as I ran downstairs shirtless in shorts. Unfortunately, I have also seen serious injuries and arrests as outcomes during these situations while I was in college. I learned some lessons as I matured and grew older, and I'd like to share some tips for young athletes getting ready to start their journeys at the next level. Of course, if you are in high school all the same advice applies.

CAMPUS LIFE QUICK TIPS:

- There are certain no-tolerance policies on nearly all campuses. Do not bring alcohol/drugs/weapons into your dorm room or on campus. Do not steal from the student union or campus store. Do not engage in any violent behavior. Do not verbally or sexually harass anyone.

- Anytime you or your teammates will be drinking alcohol, secure a safe responsible ride. Don't jeopardize anyone's safety over a poor decision. Too many lives are lost every year due to drunk drivers. The $15 spent on a ride home is nothing compared to devastating another family and your own.

- Refrain from wearing school-branded clothing or athletic gear when you are out around the town. Never tell a police officer or employee of an establishment that you are an athlete at the local university for any reason. This will only end with you making local headlines and likely making the situation worse. It is likely you are also not a local celebrity who is going to have favors pulled on your behalf.

- If a person has been drinking alcohol, stay away from engaging in any sexual behavior with them, period. Once someone has been drinking, they are not able to give legitimate consent. Respectfully turn them down. Follow up with the person the next day; if they are still interested you can pursue it further. It really is that simple and there is no grey area. It is unfortunate this has to be explained, but we still see many instances of sexual misconduct every year across college campuses.

- Enjoy the recreation that campus has to offer, network and step out of your comfortable social situation. Exploring the city's local bars and restaurants, house parties after victories, homecoming festivities, and just hanging out in the dorms or off-campus.

- Avoid "going out" or staying up too late any day of the week other than Saturday during season. Celebrating victories is a huge part of the college experience and strengthening bonds with teammates. Keep in mind while celebrating, most teams have scheduled film and lifts on Sundays even after a long travel back. You will have morning classes and early weights throughout the week. Your sleep is extremely important for your physical and mental wellbeing.

- Everything you do is a representation of your football program and self. There is a magnifying glass on you from the first day you step on campus. Don't be an idiot. Even little things can be brought to your coach's attention if someone is offended or upset with your choices.

Here are a few actions I have personally seen in my five-year career that got football players in trouble:

- Stealing a single banana from the cafeteria.

- Bringing marijuana on a road trip to an away game and smoking across the street from the hotel parking lot.

- Stealing money out of teammates' backpacks.

- Stealing jewelry from a teammate's locker.

- Getting in a fight inside a dorm room.

- Playing with a toy gun inside the dorm room.

- Swearing at a cafeteria employee.

- Having alcohol in their dorm room before going out to a party.

- Driving home drunk from a party.

- Getting involved with females sexually while intoxicated.

- Failing team drug tests.

Not all these scenarios are black and white. But at the end of the day, student-athletes are held to a certain standard, and all it takes is one headline or rumor to tarnish your reputation. Never put yourself in a situation where you are liable for another person's decision making. For example, you will likely have a teammate who smokes marijuana, a teammate who drives after drinking, a teammate who skips class, and a teammate who parties during the week. Don't let another teammate convince or give you approval to make the same poor decisions. You are better off persuading them to correct their own actions or disregarding them. These players generally aren't invested in their own success or the program's. Short-sighted vision is what leads to many of these poor decisions. Stealing that banana may save you a dollar right now, but if it costs you thousands of dollars in scholarship money you might rethink the decision. Same goes for essentially any other decision you can make– pursuing instant gratification almost always has a long-term downside or risk associated with it. While in high school my mom put up a picture outside of my bedroom with the quote, "Never give up what you want most for what you want today." The quote always particularly stuck with me while I was pushing toward graduation in college. There will always be temptations throughout life, it takes discipline to stay grounded on your path.

I have witnessed or been a part of several instances of going out to bars or parties with teammates where one small change in events could have taken someone's life or ended their career. One event took place during my senior year. We were struggling as a team, and my morale was down as well. I tried to avoid going out during the season, but this was homecoming my last year in school and I wanted to make some memories. Our senior homecoming, we lost to a top-five-ranked team in the country. We played well and had the game very competitive until halftime, however the other team just had more depth and dominated the second half. They had crazy production, something like scoring six out of the first ten plays to start the second half. Homecoming is one of those occasions where at any college campus, there are numerous social events. Doesn't matter how big or small the school is. My two roommates and I decided to go out to our local campus bar that night with several of our teammates. The night went as usual with no issue, we enjoyed some drinks, and I captivated the crowd with my moves on the dance floor. Bystanders may have a different account of my dancing ability. Once it was bar close, the night took a turn for the worse. My roommates and I were walking to the street corner to wait for our ride home. As we were walking my roommate realized he had forgotten his wallet in the bar. We decided to enter the bar through the side entrance rather than walking all the way to the main entrance. As we attempted to walk through the door we physically bumped into a group of men, who immediately seemed like they wanted trouble. Remember "Oh shit" moments? This was one of those. Situations like this happen on occasion and can usually be erased by a simple apology or ignoring it and moving on. One guy however, appeared to be looking for a fight and wasn't dropping it. In an instance of poor decision making we engaged in a shouting match with this random group. Before we could blink, two separate gentlemen came from behind us in the street. An older dude built like a refrigerator sucker punched me in the jaw from the side. As I spun around, I saw him punching my other roommate, knocking my roommate's cowboy hat off of his head. I turned around to get my bearings, and saw the group that attacked us were all running away into the parking lot. I saw my third roommate down the street completely covered in blood. A woman with the group had smashed a full-size bottle against the side of my roommate's head and sliced his face from above the eyebrow down to the nose. Both of my roommates were over 6'2" and 240 pound collegiate defensive lineman. This scenario showed all of us, you never know who you could be dealing with. It is best to avoid confrontation at any costs. You can always walk away. That night it was a bottle, but it could have easily been a gun. My roommate ended up needing several stitches and had to go through concussion protocol, but luckily that was all. It would not have been crazy to have been blinded by that type of attack. That could have easily been myself and could have abruptly ended my senior season. No one wants to experience an unfortunate ending to their athletic career like that. My roommate did return that season and finished strong. He was one of the toughest players I ever had the pleasure of playing with. This guy had a sprained MCL, stitches/concussion, and broken hand all in the same season while finishing second on the team in sacks. That's persevering through difficult situations. I never once heard him complain or carry a victim mindset.

This is one scenario, although there are videos on social media, and headlines across the country where confrontations become deadly all the time. Everyone has seen the national headlines with NFL players involved in domestic violence, or collegiate athletes involved in drunken mischief. These are mistakes that will stay with those individuals for the rest of their life.

As an athlete, people may target you and attack your status for no reason at times. They will feel they can speak to your however they want, attempting to see how you react. I have witnessed scenarios where people pull guns out or grab a weapon because they are intimidated by the size of another person as an example. You just never know what is going to happen. Always go out with people you trust, who can look out for you, but at the same time are going to avoid getting in trouble. You can certainly go out and have a good time, just be sure to always keep the thought in the back of your head. "Don't do anything to hurt yourself, your family, or this football team." Ultimately, life is all about decisions. As we've discussed, intent is the motive for every decision we make. What is your intent when you are going out? Are you looking for trouble? Looking for girls? Looking to get drunk? If this is what you are looking for, you may need to reevaluate your stance as an athlete and person.

I don't want to sound like you have to be anxious or worried about enjoying your life. I had countless nights of entertainment and good memories that went without drama. I've seen many hilarious instances of drunk debauchery that involved no one getting hurt. Freshman chugging milk until they puke, many feats of manliness, hilarious dance moves, debuting a teammate's rap single at a party, random drunk sports challenges, costume parties, the list is endless. Some of the best nights in college are spent sitting in a random basement or backyard having a few drinks and enjoying quality time with your teammates and friends. There will hopefully be many more positive experiences than negative ones. The reason for highlighting negative experiences is because they tend to leave a heavier impact on your development. Nights of mistakes become learning and growing opportunities. There are countless positive aspects to campus life as well.

Utilize the clubs and organizations on campus to build connections and expose yourself to different opportunities. I was able to go to my first NFL game as a result of a job opportunity partnered with our Criminal Justice and Sociology Club. I ended up working field-level security following the camera crew for the Vikings on the New Year's Day game. I got paid $25 an hour and had an experience most people will probably never get to live. I met the Head Coach of the youth football team I help coach through a job fair, who happened to be an alumnus of my university and a member of the football team years before. We connected, and he invited me to coach with him. There are people always looking to help college students, and many times these individuals partner with clubs on campus, providing them exclusive opportunities or knowledge. Not only do extra-curriculars build a strong resume, they offer chances outside of athletics to be a part of something important on campus. I have played with a few teammates who are presidents or key members of on-campus organizations. These guys always end up getting awesome jobs after graduation. Not due to the fact they were in a club, but because of the character traits and habits they carry into their mindset.

Many of the lifelong relationships and memories you make as an athlete will be far away from the playing field. I had the pleasure of meeting my current girlfriend while I was in community college. Bless her brave soul, she moved across the country to keep us together. More on that story later. I have friends all over the country from playing football and I've had the pleasure of meeting many amazing people who have made me a better person. Going out and spending time with your teammates is a direct way of building team chemistry. In college you will have the opportunity to meet people from very different backgrounds and be exposed to different political beliefs, cultures, and lifestyles than your own. This is a blessing and allows for a large window of personal development and growth. It is important to get out of you comfort zone to experience these connections. You won't make new friends staying in your dorm room every night playing video games. I asked my good friend Jamar Pinnock to touch on his experience of campus life as an athlete. Jamar was in my freshman class at junior college and we were in the same position group. Jamar went from being unrecruited out of high school to playing for Youngstown State University and playing in the FCS National Championship game within four years. He graduated with his degree in General Studies and currently sells insurance in Phoenix. He had this to say when I asked him to write about his experience during college:

"What's the experience like playing at a Division I school? That's a question I always asked myself.

The Division I experience I must say is a tremendous experience. All the new gear you get, staying in beautiful hotels before the games, playing in front of thousands of people, never having to worry about where your next meal will come from, the list goes on and on. Not to mention getting your degree paid for, which is the main objective.

The Division I one experience is great, but it also comes with a lot of distractions. Imagine having to not ever worry about paying for classes, eating good, and getting a lot of attention from the ladies. You have access to all the best parties and all those things that might come to mind when you think of being a college athlete. All those are extremely fun, don't get me wrong, but those distractions can also have you explaining to your parents or loved ones why you aren't playing next year because you couldn't stay focused. This is a terrible feeling to think about. Some athletes get so caught up in the lifestyle, they forget the main reasons why they are at school in the first place. What's the ultimate dream for any college athlete? If you ask me, I would say playing professionally and making a living playing the sport you love. Of course, there's also walking away with that degree as a personal accomplishment and being prepared for life after football, because we all know the storm can strike at any moment.

I've never played professionally, but I've been around special athletes who worked their tail off to get to the next level. One thing I always admired about these guys is that they always put the extra work in, and they always kept their eyes on the prize despite the distractions. Now I'm not going to sit here and make those guys seem like the perfect athletes, never going out and just working out all the time. However, they knew when it was work time and when to put the bullshit aside. On the night of the 2016 NFL draft myself and a couple teammates had the opportunity to watch our former teammates get drafted. A couple others signed free agent contracts which was exciting. One thing I kept hearing after the draft was "If he got picked up, I know I can get picked up," or, "Man, it's on now, I'm really about to start getting this work." My thoughts toward those comments was why weren't they putting in the work before? Did they not know it takes extra work to even get a chance at that level? It was not surprising that those comments came from my teammates who enjoyed everything the campus life had to offer a little too much. They thought they had it all figured out, but they didn't realize that it's crucial what you do with your time. While you're sitting around wasting your time, there are athletes out there not skipping a step."

Whether you are a Division I or junior college athlete, there will always be distractions. The decision lies on yourself as a student-athlete to be a positive role-model on campus and in the community. There will be plenty of memories and lifelong bonds formed during your college years. These memories don't have to be coupled with nights of horrible outcomes. You can enjoy all the positive aspects of campus life without ever having to experience a single negative one. It begins with intent and decision making. If you make the right decisions and take pride in your character as a person, you will avoid having any issues. Always remember you can walk away from any situation. Don't lose the opportunity you worked your entire life for over seconds of anger, sadness, or poor judgement.

5
FINANCES AND JOBS

UNDOUBTEDLY, ONE OF the biggest struggles college students face across the nation is financial instability. Student-athletes are perceived as being the exception to this due to the glorified nature of athletic scholarships. This couldn't be further from the reality of the situation. In recent years, certain stories have gained national media attention highlighting this issue. High-profile programs have been outed for assisting in paying utility bills of players' family members. Former players have come out and admitted to accepting money from boosters to help pay rent and avoid going to bed hungry. Research conducted in previous years found average out-of-pocket expenses for a full-ride Division I athlete to be upwards of $3,000. Furthermore, over 80% of student athletes studied were found to be living in poverty. During junior college, it was not uncommon to find two-bedroom apartments near campus with up to eight teammates living in them. After transferring, I found the situation to be similar living with up to nine people in our house at one point. If you are able to avoid it, I would never recommend living with eight roommates in a one bathroom house. For many student-athletes, chasing your dreams will come with a price during your career. Financial struggles are a nearly inevitable part of the college experience for most students. However, with a few key tips and pieces of information, all student-athletes can help themselves out and take some burden from their shoulders.

Money rules the world, and it is no different whether you are a student athlete or Bill Gates. I secured my first job the same week I turned fourteen, bussing tables at a local Italian restaurant in my hometown. One of the first nights I was working, without ever being trained, a server asked me to bring out eight waters to a table on the patio. I filled up the glasses of water and placed them on a server's tray. My hands started shaking as I carried the tray with both hands out to the patio. I attempted to take the waters off and place them in front of each guest. I didn't understand the process of removing the waters opposite of each other to keep the tray balanced. I started taking the first few waters from the right side of the tray, and before I knew it, I had spilled six waters in the lap of an elderly woman, drenching her and the table. I can never erase the image from my mind of her smiling at me saying, "It's okay, sweetie, it is quite hot out here anyways." The server wasn't quite as understanding of my mistake. Working was always a part of my life after that point, though it wasn't looked at as a punishment, requirement, or accomplishment. I was taught that's just what you did: you got up, went to school, then went to work. On the reverse side, I played football with teammates that graduated college without ever having a job. Whether you are fortunate enough to come from a family background where your parents can assist in supporting you, or you are entirely on your own, I would advocate for everyone to get a job during high school and college. There are plenty of different ways to make money. Entering the work force builds strong skills that transfer to success in athletics and life. For reference, here is a list of jobs I have held at the age of 22:

- Busboy

- Dishwasher

- Pizza Delivery Driver

- Newspaper Delivery Customer Service

- Telemarketer

- Truck Unloader and Shelf Stocker

- Painter

- Line Cook

- Security

- Food Runner

- Counselor at Youth Homeless/Juvenile Shelter

- After-School Teacher in Non-Profit Organization

- Program Coordinator for After-School Care Program

In high school I was working mostly as a dishwasher, where I learned more about work ethic than any other job in comparison. I opened and closed a country club restaurant every Saturday and Sunday through my entire senior football season. Whether we got back from the bus ride at 1 AM, or it was the morning after homecoming, I would be at the restaurant at 7 AM. I typically worked between 24-28 hours over the course of the weekend. This meant I was getting paid around $500 every two weeks. This was an absurd amount of money as a high schooler with no real living expenses. The money was well earned. I once spent an entire slow summer day scrubbing the walls of the kitchen with a toothbrush. The job had its ups and downs, but I had a few memorable experiences. I typically worked with an older gentleman in the dish pit in the summer and spring seasons. He was in his 50's, and at times difficult to understand with his thick Jamaican accent. We got along well and usually spent time talking about sports or music. One day I had been instructed to take out the fryer and replace the oil. I had no idea what that meant, but I figured it was self-explanatory considering no one had taught me how. I rolled the fryer out to the back and began to pour all the piping hot oil down the regular drainage system. It began to overflow and spill out into the parking lot. This was another classic "Oh Shit" moment. I went to go ask the other dishwasher to come check it out. He immediately began mumbling every swear word imaginable, exclaiming we were in huge trouble. This guy was stressing wiping the beads of sweat off his forehead, while I was still extremely confused. The executive chef came outside and saw it, his face was priceless. He was absolutely furious, evident by his facial expression. I think he also realized whoever told me to dump the oil without training me was as much of an idiot as I was. He told me to go get a bucket with soapy water and the push broom. I had to clean the entire parking lot where the oil had dripped as it was now incredibly slippery for the guests entering the restaurant. He then showed me the waste container for the oil, which was ten feet to my right, the size of a small vehicle, and labeled "OIL WASTE CONTAINER" in large letters on the side. Whoops. I learned a lot over the course of my few years at that job and saved up more money than I knew what to do with. My last story from that job has a better ending. Once after a fancy wedding, we had a very detailed ice sculpture that had been carved by our very own executive chef. This chef was not very popular in the kitchen amongst the staff, and I particularly was not a fan of his. He once threatened to beat me up in the basement. As we were closing the restaurant, our line cook bet me ten bucks that I wouldn't be able to throw the ice sculpture over the wall in the back of the restaurant. I gladly accepted and won the bet. We told the chef the next morning that we dropped it by accident while moving it. Now those were some good times!

Aside from all the growth and memorable experiences, the money earned from all my jobs in high school directly helped further my athletic career. I can't tell you how many kids I talk to that say they can't afford protein powder, cleats, or a college camp to get recruited. I follow with asking them if they have a job, where they typically respond, "I don't have time with school and sports." As a generation of millennial athletes, we need to move away from this being an acceptable and reasonable answer. You have time, you just don't want to work and make money as bad as you act like you do. Playing video games, partying, sleeping in, and hanging out with friends typically place higher on the list of importance in comparison to securing a job for many kids. I managed to work back-to-back doubles every weekend throughout my senior year of high school, while also spending time with my girlfriend. I would typically get off around 10 PM, drive to my girlfriend's house and stay up until 2 or 3 AM, then wake up and drive back to the restaurant after changing. This wasn't smart, but I'm alive. I survived. You are certainly able to sacrifice at least one day a week to working.

The savings went toward my trainer, supplements and extra food, and gas/miscellaneous expenses. Since I was living with my parents at the time I still had food and no other bills. I may have taken my girlfriend to eat at my favorite restaurant far more than I should have, but I was comfortable. When I ran out of protein, I bought some more. If I wanted to get a new piece of training equipment, I ordered it. I eventually used the money from over the years, about five thousand in total, to move out on my own after my first two years of community college. The rest of the time during college I was using my paychecks to pay for all my bills and living expenses. My parents assisted me throughout college financially and always helped when I needed it. I was blessed in that regard. Money was always tight still as a student, and there was no point during college where I could walk in to a store and just buy things that I wanted. There was always a rhyme and reason. As you grow older you will realize how crucial it is to practice strong spending habits and saving money. While in college, your budget will vary depending on your cost of living and the area your school is located in.

FINANCE AND JOBS QUICK TIPS:

- Get a job as early as possible and put away money while your bills are minimal to none. Spend money on investing in yourself as an athlete and person (training, personal equipment, nutrition, gym membership, education, books, health products).

- Pay your bills first and accrue as little debt as possible. Set monthly limits for recreational money and track your expenses using a notepad on your phone. Each month, designate the three expenses which could be cut back on.

- Avoid spending money on: clothes, eating out, unnecessary material items, and avoidable mistakes (parking tickets/speeding tickets/late fees, etc.) Too many times I have seen my teammates buying expensive clothes while struggling to eat a decent meal.

- Apply for jobs that can give you relevant experience in your career field when possible. Network with professionals and display your work ethic and skills to build strong connections that can be used after graduation.

- Only take out as many student loans as necessary. Never take out extra loans to receive a larger refund check; any student loan will have to be paid back in full, except for a few circumstances. Any time you borrow money, you will be paying it back with interest added on top of the original amount borrowed.

- Begin building credit by applying for a credit card early. I did not get a credit card until after graduation. I could have been building my credit during college simply by using a credit card for bills and gas. If you do not qualify for a specific card right away, investigate into college student cards. Once you are approved for a credit card, use it responsibly and pay off the amount in full every month. It can be very easy to accrue credit card debt with irresponsible spending habits.

- Before you purchase anything, ask yourself two questions: Do I want or need this? If you need it, can it be purchased for cheaper? This will quickly answer whether a purchase is justifiable in most cases.

You have several different types of student loans for athletes who are not on full scholarship, and it is important to note and know the differences between each of them. You will have federal subsidized and unsubsidized loans, as well as private loans from different vendors. The financial aid office will be your best friend in explaining the differences between each. Student loan debt is a crippling problem within the US economy, with 44.2 million people suffering from it. Whether you are a walk-on, or on a full ride, your mindset needs to be tailored toward minimizing debt. Understanding how you pay back your loans, what the interest rates will be, how long the grace period is, and if you are eligible for loan forgiveness are all a part of the process of financial stability. Developing strong financial habits should begin well before college.

While you are in high school, you should aim to put away a set amount of money each pay period that you will save for college. Whether it is 50 or 100 dollars, it will add up over time after one to three years of working. This money should not be touched and could even be put into a separate bank account. The remaining majority of your money should go toward extra food, as well as a gym membership. While you are working hard for your money, don't be afraid to spend it on a personal "want" or entertainment as appropriate. Just don't get carried away and remember to stay focused on the long-term vision. Set concrete, measurable limits for yourself to adjust good spending habits:

- Eat out once a week.

- Spend money on entertainment twice a month (movie, going out, bowling, dates).

These will be easy for you to see if you are failing or meeting the expectations you have set for yourself. If you go through your monthly budget as discussed and see you are spending 50% of the money you make on video games and clothes, you can easily identify where the problem is. Without a system of tracking, you will simply look at your bank account in confusion wondering why you're not saving as much money as you expected to.

While in college as a student athlete, your options for work will be heavily limited due to schedule constraints. This does not mean there aren't plenty of readily available jobs. When it comes to job opportunities, and deciding where to work, these are a few guidelines I suggest for athletes in college:

DO's:

- Get a service job that pays tips and has flexible scheduling.

- Invest in careers/fields that are relevant to your major as a junior and senior.

- Make connections at jobs to return after the season if you have the interest in doing so.

- Look for jobs as close as possible to campus to eliminate commutes and make scheduling easier.

Recommended:

- Food Service (bussing/food running/serving), Security (venue/event regular hours), Sales, Customer Service (retail stores).

DON'T's:

- Avoid physical labor jobs during the season/and or summer. I unloaded trucks in the morning my freshman year of junior college during the summer and I was worn out physically before 8 AM.

Wearing yourself out at work will of course make workouts and training more difficult. My senior year I still hadn't learned my lesson and got a job running food at Stella's Fish Café in Uptown Minneapolis. Normally, food running is a great option for athletes. But at Stella's, the rooftop patio was one of the most popular places to eat in the summer- which required the staff, including myself, to carry food up seven flights of stairs. I didn't realize how awful this would be until after I started. This process ran essentially non-stop for four or five hours during a shift. My legs were conditioned, but ultimately grew tired and were never really allowed the opportunity to get the rest they needed.

• Avoid jobs where you are sitting for eight hours straight. It may seem like a smart idea to relax, but remember you are an athlete. Sitting in a chair for long periods of time will tighten your muscles and cause tension in your body. Ideally you can work a job in the middle ground between physically exhausting and stagnant.

• Don't work a job that will have extreme hours. Bouncing and working security at bars is very popular amongst collegiate athletes, however this throws a wrench in your sleep schedule. If you are only able to sleep a few hours before morning workouts and expect an afternoon nap to solve the problem, you are wrong. You will be exhausted while training and losing out on the benefits.

- Don't apply for jobs that are primarily outside. Your body will be outside for conditioning and field work, so you should avoid over exposure to the sun and heat in the summer months by working inside.

Caution:

- Landscaping, Call Centers, Kitchen Jobs, Construction, Fast Food.

These are just guidelines. At the end of the day you will have to do what you need to do to survive and be comfortable. I have had teammates who worked two jobs during the season while sleeping for a few hours a night. Not every campus and city will have the same amount of job opportunities. If you are in a rural community, physical labor jobs may be easier to come by. Part of growing up and maturing is embracing the fact that you are going to have to work to provide yourself an income. That is the reality of the situation. Keeping in mind that maybe one person on your team will have an opportunity to play professionally, you shouldn't shy away from working because you carry the dream of getting paid to play your sport.

As you progress through college, you want to shift the perspective of working from a "means of survival" to "What do I want to do for the rest of my life?" At the latest, by your junior year you should be developing a professional resume. Identify what types of jobs you would like to have on your resume and how they will benefit you in your future. I essentially graduated with a degree and zero relevant experience. I applied for probably 100 positions before getting an internship for thirteen dollars an hour with my bachelor's degree. The job was a residential counselor position at a shelter for juvenile and homeless teenagers. I had to commute thirty minutes and work a rotating schedule including weekends. It wasn't a glamorous situation, but I understood it was necessary to continue to grow, and I was grateful for the opportunity. Invest in yourself and build for your future early. Don't be afraid to cold-call and email companies you have an interest in. Sometimes a strong candidate can generate interest in a company to create a part-time position or internship opportunity. Many companies can work around your schedule if you can sell yourself as a strong fit. The experience and connections gained through working will be valuable once you are looking for a full-time position after graduation.

Finances can be stressful and certainly add a lot to the plate of an already overwhelmed college student. Be sure to occasionally take a step back, take a deep breath, and lean on whatever support system you have– don't be afraid to ask for help. Most college campuses will have a career services center where you can make an appointment for free advice regarding a resume, interview tips, and job openings. Reach out to your head coach for alumni connections who may be in the community still running businesses. Use every networking opportunity available– you must develop relationships. Securing a career is ultimately the primary reason you are attending school. Many of my former teammates struggled with motivating themselves in the classroom, while simultaneously claiming they will be rich in a few years. The harsh truth is, most of these teammates were the ones who got smacked in the face with reality after college. Some failed to graduate. The characteristics of financially successful people are directly comparable to those of strong athletes and students. This begins with seeking meaningful employment as a student. Having a job that either supplies a strong source of income, or one that excites your interests is a key tool for motivation in the classroom.

Many employers recently are trending toward recruiting former athletes. It is not uncommon to find popular job recruitment websites with lists such as "Top Twenty Jobs for Former Athletes." A quick google search will turn up articles such as "Seven Reasons You Should Hire Athletes" as top results. This is essentially creating a new niche market of opportunities for athletes in specific fields. Hiring managers are searching for many of the qualities athletes possess such as discipline, time-management, leadership, work-ethic, and perseverance. It is important to utilize this to your advantage as a student-athlete. Whether you are cooking in the cafeteria or completing a rigorous summer internship at a Fortune 500 company, you are exponentially better off in comparison to the unemployed student. Implement the resources and techniques that are accessible to branch out and find the opportunity you are dreaming of.

6
TRAINING AND NUTRITION

THE MOST COMMONLY asked question young athletes and football players ask me is "How do I get bigger and faster?" or "Can you give me any workout advice?". These are both valid questions, with in-depth answers. There is no doubt that training and nutrition are some of the single most valuable pieces of knowledge any athlete can possess. As I was preparing to head into high school, I was 5'4" and 115 pounds. At the time, I really thought I was a Division I football player. I was smacked in the face physically on the field, and mentally after my disappointing freshman season. That season I wasn't a starter for the first time in my entire life. While already being the youngest kid in my class, I made the decision to no longer also be the smallest. I never missed a workout the rest of my athletic career. I was determined to grow stronger and become a better athlete. I used to spend every waking second of my day watching YouTube videos and reading articles on how to jump higher, run faster, and gain explosiveness. The first piece of advice I will give in this section goes back to topics discussed earlier: Great athletes make decisions with the intent to be great. That does not only mean deciding to go and put in some extra field work, but also focusing on putting in *quality* field work. If it means preparing meals on Sunday night to eat lunch during class, that's what has to be done. I had former teammates who would skip weight training during junior college because they didn't want to go to class sweaty. You can't make this stuff up. I don't have to tell you that these guys did not turn out to be successful athletes. They usually quit or bounced from program to program, blaming everyone but themselves for their struggles.

TRAINING QUICK TIPS:

- As an athlete you should at a minimum be on the field as many hours a week as you're in the weight room. I would argue that ideally you should be on the field five days a week and lifting three to four times.

- Research how the professionals train and model it, do not try to recreate the wheel. Stick to the basics. There have been thousands of academic studies performed to validate the most successful methods of training.

- If possible find a professional skill trainer to pay for a few sessions a week so you can separate yourself from your competition. Search social media and the internet for trainers that charge reasonable prices. I trained with Airabin Justin and Showtyme Performance in high school and junior college. Undoubtedly, this provided the most progression in my athletic development. I had essentially hit my ceiling as far as my training and knowledge of the game had gone. Airabin provided experience from a former professional player and educated me on the nuances of the game while also improving my speed and technique.

- You will have to add onto whatever diet your parents and school provide with additional calories and supplements to maximize your results and recovery. Going to the store and buying cheap, quality items that you can add to your diet is crucial for any athlete to reach their full potential.

- As a broke and hungry athlete there will be times where you will compromise tasty food for convenience and availability. There were times I would eat ketchup on white rice as a meal. People would comment saying it looked disgusting. Truth is, it didn't taste very good, but it was easy, quick, and inexpensive for me to prepare. The grind of being an athlete isn't always glamorous.

- Invest in simple tools to take care of your body at home: foam roller, exercise band (for stretching), tennis ball, Epsom salt, and ice. Recovery becomes more important the further you progress into your athletic career. The guys who never get injured are the ones doing injury prevention after and before workouts.

- If you decide to skip working out, be prepared to spend extra time in the training room when you inevitably get injured. I've seen it happen time and time again. The guys who get injured are the ones who miss workouts consistently.

- The single biggest component of training is effort! I don't care if you're following the most scientifically proven, most advanced training regimen in the world. Training programs, equipment, and facilities are all meaningless without championship-level effort. The kid training in his tennis shoes at the park can get more out of a workout than the kid with $200 cleats and an NFL trainer in an air-conditioned facility. Walter Payton, one of the all-time great NFL running backs, used to run hills in the deltas of Mississippi to improve his speed in the offseason. When questioned about how he approached conditioning in the off-season Walter Payton replied, "I try to kill myself. I work myself out to the extent where when I'm through I can't walk." That's a perfect example of making the most out of the most universally available resource, effort. Every training session is an opportunity to permanently become a better athlete, so treat it as such.

- Try to find a training partner who will hold you accountable and push you to be better. I trained frequently with a few good buddies of mine, Steven Hubick and Jamar Pinnock. We did not allow each other to cheat reps, take breaks, or get distracted. Training with a partner will also have you relying on your partner for attendance if you need each other for throwing the ball, partner drills, rides, etc.

As you go through school it is important to develop a plan for your training through the year. Waking up and saying to yourself, *I think I'm going to go hoop today*, is not making the best use of your time. Multi-sport athletes in high school will be limited in their options for training depending on the sport and season. If you are a three-sport athlete, you will essentially have only the summer to devote entirely to football. I would highly recommend wrestling, track, or basketball as a 2nd sport, and staying away from a third in most instances. Two sports are great for skill development, however a third really limits your ability to develop a full off-season program and dedicate yourself to the sport you would like to compete in in college. I participated in football, wrestling, and baseball as a freshman in high school, and I enjoyed it. I attended a smaller high school, and this was standard for many of our athletes. It was easy and comfortable to kind of "get by" being in season year-round. I eventually realized I was not where I wanted to be as a football player if I really wanted to play at the next level. My father's favorite sport was baseball, and he believed it to be my best sport as well. I walked into the baseball coach's office before my sophomore season and let him know I wouldn't be playing. He probably laughed in his head as I explained my goals of playing college football after not starting on junior varsity as a freshman. I was extremely nervous to break the news to my father, who really didn't care once it was done. He was supportive of my goal to play football in college. The time I gained to train for football was mandatory for my development. The following training advice will be assuming you are not currently competing in another sport as an athlete. For college athletes, this applies mostly to mindset and preparation.

Field Work/Speed Work/Agility Work:

This is the most critical part of becoming a better athlete. The weight room gives you strength to be able to move more explosively; however, getting on the field and working on your craft is how you develop the ability to use that strength. Early in my career I had what most people would define as a meathead mentality. We all know the guy in the locker room who can bench press more than many of the participants at the NFL combine, yet they don't play on gameday. That was me, able to bench press 225 pounds for over 20 reps as a sophomore in college while playing cornerback. These guys may or may not be one of the better athletes on the team. I know for myself, when I spent the majority of my time in the weight room, I became stiff and immobile on the field. This did not translate to the success I thought it would. Regardless of how much stronger or bigger I got, I still found myself on the sidelines early in my career. I had this obsession with gaining size and growing stronger, however I was riding the bench and getting injured often. The second I backed off on weightlifting and directed the extra time to working out on the field, I started seeing results in practice. The sand pit, hill sprints, turf, grass, dirt, and pavement all made me a much better athlete! I was outside, moving fast, moving explosively, moving with intent, and visualizing making the plays in my head. I was working out with a purpose. I would recommend a variety of different workouts to switch things up and keep your skill set balanced. Here is how I would break down the different environments and their uses and benefits:

The field – Where you make plays. Your second bedroom. The field should become so familiar you could drive or walk to it blindfolded. On the field you practice your fundamentals, technique, and ball skills. If you neglect the field, you will feel it come the start of the season.

The track – a lot of football players stay away from the track because you can sprint on the football field. I disagree and see the track as a different environment where your mindset changes. When you are working out on the track it is purely for speed development. Get yourself a cheap pair of track spikes and focus on sprinting. I would usually workout on the track at least once a week. I performed sets of measured sprints no longer than forty yards focused on improving my top-end speed and acceleration.

The sand – This environment is for a change of pace and not always readily available. Most campuses have a sand pit for volleyball, or a local park, weather permitting. As a defensive back I loved hitting the sand pit and tightening my footwork up. Sand training has been linked to increased plyometric training efficiency in comparison to hard ground. In addition, training in sand has also shown a decrease in muscle soreness post workout. Go in there barefoot and improve your foot speed, conditioning, and balance. Sand is where you focus on explosive movements. Sprinting in sand will alter the mechanics you use when sprinting on the field and can be detrimental. When working out in sand, you will feel the bottoms of your feet getting exhausted. As an athlete you spend all day on your feet, but so many people neglect them during training and recovery.

The pavement – This is where there are no excuses. I kept at bare minimum a pair of tennis shoes, cones, resistance bands, and an agility ladder in my car at all times. This prevented me from skipping any workout I was planning for. If it was raining? I had the garage. Gym was closed? Had the parking lot. Sand pit has a volleyball tournament? The sidewalk was available. The pavement is available anywhere, anytime, and always provides an opportunity for a workout. No longer is the excuse "I don't have a field near my house" acceptable.

The hill – The hill is a primary tool for speed training, but it also adds a different dynamic: mental toughness. Steven and I used to hit the hill in 100+ degree weather. It was almost like we were just waiting for someone to tap out first. Those were some of the best workouts, because we pushed each other past our limits.

As a young athlete I would recommend familiarizing yourself with each of these different environments and putting a plan in place. There is never an excuse to not get some work in. Continuing with these training places, we will dive into the equipment you can add into your workouts. First of all, the only thing you absolutely need is cleats or shoes. There were hundreds of times where I worked out without even as much as a line on the ground. Of course, if you are able to add some materials to your workout that are beneficial, you should.

Cones – I would recommend every athlete has two packs of cones in their backpack or car. These can help you set up simple drills, simulate lines, and serve as visual aids. Cones are excellent to create landmarks for consistency. If you have no lines on a field, cones can offer your sprints and drills the chance to be consistent. They are also the cheapest piece of equipment any athlete can purchase.

Agility Ladder – This is a huge topic of controversial discussion in the football training community. I used to do ladder drills more religiously than I brushed my teeth. I also had lightning-fast footwork– however, it was not because of the ladders. Ladders should be used as a warmup or finisher for conditioning. I used to do ladder drills in between repetitions of my dynamic warmup. They will increase your foot speed and decrease contact time with the ground, but also enforce bad habits such as looking down and shortening your range of motion. Do not rely on ladders to improve your football skill, this is one of the biggest mistakes young athletes are making today. Replicate movements you will perform in a game instead. Ladders can be a helpful tool only if used correctly.

Resistance Bands – Essential for stretching, also a great device to implement resisted movements and dynamic partner drills in your workouts. Resistance bands are handy for active rest days to extend your range of motion while stretching. I frequently used resistance bands around my ankles during footwork drills to strengthen my hips and practice body control.

Jump rope – Conditioning and warming up. One of the simplest and most effective tools that has been used forever.

Football – Do not go on the field and go through drills over and over without incorporating the most essential part of a football game.

Some commonly used equipment that is a waste of money and should be disregarded includes mini hurdles and parachutes. There is nothing these pieces of equipment offer that can't be replicated for free. Parachutes can actually enforce bad habits while sprinting due to the parachute pulling each side of your body disproportionately.

Efficient powerful movement is the focus of all training as an athlete. You should not be focusing solely on strength or weight, but more importantly how explosively and smoothly you are moving. How quickly will your body react when you make a mistake? How well is it physically able to? Research specific position drills based on your skill level and position on the field. There are plenty of amazing resources available online to find drills for any position. Instagram and YouTube offer free videos from many credible trainers. Begin to practice introductory drills until you perfect them and then add degrees of difficulty. Avoid fancy workouts that are flashy and fail to accomplish much. I cringe when I think back to some of the drills I used to do while training. I was chopping my feet for twenty seconds moving in all sorts of directions, accomplishing nothing. I would then post them on Instagram with rap music playing. Don't do what I did. The average football play lasts a few seconds. If you are going through a matrix of ladders and cones while spinning around in circles, you are wasting your time and effort. There is a distinct difference between a movement that translates to the field and one that doesn't. It doesn't make sense for an offensive lineman to spend all their time on the football field practicing their backpedal or vertical jump.

Do not ever neglect the effects of competing and field-time. The athlete who spends all summer playing pick-up 7-on-7 and working out on the field will benefit more than the athlete who lived in the weight room and gained a bunch of strength. During my first few years of college, I was a perfect example of how *not* to approach training. My freshman year I remember certain players were constantly on the field. Always running routes, always wanting to throw the ball around. I found it silly, because I didn't know any better. I thought that if I couldn't bench press an arbitrary number, I wouldn't be a great football player. After focusing most of my time and energy toward lifting weights, I had spent most of my entire first two seasons on the sideline or injured. I eventually came to the realization that defensive backs rarely utilize the bench press movement in a game. At the same time, most of the players who started in front of me and succeeded didn't focus as much on their lifts. In fact, a study conducted on Division I football players focused on tracking strength, speed, and body composition changes over a playing career found several skill position freshmen who were unable to bench press 225 pounds initially upon reporting to campus. Many young athletes might find this information simply unbelievable, but this is the reality on every campus. Athletes getting recruited to compete in college are the best performers, not necessarily the strongest players. Every year there are guys sitting on their couch, who can lift a whole tone of weight, wishing they could play football. I played with a receiver by the name of Teddy Ruben during junior college. Teddy was not much bigger than 5'10" and 170 pounds, however he went on to become an All-Conference Receiver and Returner at Troy University. Teddy was one of the guys always on the field, always working on his craft. I'm sure I was stronger than Teddy while I was a freshman and he was a redshirt sophomore, but I damn sure couldn't cover him very well, as he was an elite route runner. He beat me so bad on one of my first 1-on-1 repetitions during practice; as he blew past me I grabbed him and dragged him to the ground to prevent a completion. The offensive coach running the drill told me to, "Get the fuck off the field and get him a defensive back who knew how to play football." Good times. Anas Hasic was another player I distinctly remember as being on the field every single day running routes, and he was another one of my junior college teammates who had the opportunity to play professionally. Both these guys always showed up to the weight room and gave phenomenal effort. The difference was, they understood that wasn't what would get them a scholarship.

Blessed to Announce

They made sure to reinforce all the work they put in the weight room with grinding on the field to perfect their craft.

Once I transferred, this theme remained consistent. During my junior year, we were given Mondays off during the season. This was the only day of the week where there were no football activities. A small group of guys were always on the field putting in extra work on that day off. On the offensive side of the ball, there were typically a few players out there. Darius Chapes, our team captain and lone all-conference offensive player, and Alquawn Vickers, an All-American return specialist. There were many more players who stuck to the theme of consistently putting in extra work on the field during my playing career, but the few highlighted happened to leave a lasting impression on me. The track records of these players speak for themselves. Nothing replaces sport-specific experience and repetition. Think back to your childhood: you were out on the field, the pavement, and at the park playing sports with whoever you could find from the neighborhood. Chances are if you are reading this you were the kid where your parent had to physically drag you to the car because you wouldn't leave. I remember playing basketball in the pouring rain for hours and not even thinking twice about it as a kid. As you grow older and progress through athletics it can be easy to get caught up in measurables such as the bench press and forty-yard-dash. While these are important, they will never replace the fundamental aspect of competing in your sport. I challenge all athletes to reflect on their attitude toward sports as a child and implement it into their current career. As a kid, if you were anything like me, when you didn't have a great game on Saturday you wouldn't head over to the gym. You would instead lace up your cleats and go in the backyard or to the local park and continue to play your sport. The downside to sport-specific training is, you can certainly hit a ceiling once your own knowledge catches up to your training level. Working out with a skill trainer, mentor, or coach can be a crucial step in the development of any young athlete preparing for college.

As mentioned previously, I started paying for a trainer during the summer heading into my senior year. I went on Google and searched "football trainers Phoenix" and blindly reached out to several by email. Airabin Justin, founder of Showtyme Performance, was the first to respond back. His response was brief: "I'll be at North Canyon at 4 on the track." That same day I got in my car and made the 25-minute drive. I showed up to the school for the first training session wearing Vans while holding my pair of cleats. Airabin looked at me and said, "You didn't bring any running shoes?" I just sort of shrugged, having no idea what to expect since I had never participated in a formal training session. Airabin took off his shoes and let me wear them as he led me through warmup drills on the track. What proceeded was the most difficult workout of my life. He whooped my ass. The first training session made me realize a few things:

1. I was not nearly as skilled as I thought I was.

2. I wasn't pushing myself to my limits when working out by myself.

3. I lacked a ton of knowledge about training and football as a sixteen-year-old.

Who knew. A year later Airabin and I would often reminisce and laugh at the fact I hadn't been able to perform the simple drills he put me through that first day. The patented warm-up included 600 yards of backpedals. I watched many kids show up to train and never come back after those backpedals. A few didn't even finish their first day. Ayrius was Airabin's brother, and the two of them consistently filmed us athletes throwing up on the side of the track to post to social media as they laughed. They knew how to push your limits in an effective manner. The frustration showed in their voices if you didn't perform to the best of your ability; they were truly invested in your success as an athlete. Airabin and Ayrius provided knowledge of the game and professional playing experience I simply didn't get from my high school coaches. I paid them with the money from my dishwashing job, and they became invaluable to my development as an athlete. Their training helped me go from not starting as a junior in high school, to breaking seven school records and earning every accolade I had hoped for as a senior. If you are fortunate enough to find a trainer that can serve as a coach and mentor, you will forever be thankful for their service. I know I would not have ever reached the levels of athletics I competed at without the guidance and support of Airabin and Ayrius. Any athlete looking to bring their game to the next level can take the same step by simply doing a few minutes of research online or on social media. I want to emphasize that it isn't necessary to have a trainer to succeed by any means. Some high schools are fortunate to have the resources for strength and conditioning coaches as well as a coaching staff with NFL alumni. This just isn't the case for many athletes, however. Hiring a trainer is a step you can control as an athlete to separate yourself from other players in your conference. I was the only person in my program who invested time, money, and energy into training outside of the required attendance from our high school program. While the most important aspect of training for any athlete is performed on the field, the weight room is still an extremely valuable tool. The best athletes can move efficiently and quickly while also having the strength to bully their opponents. All time in the weight room is not spent equally, and more is not always better. There are a couple important pieces to remember while lifting as an athlete.

I loved the weight room for a couple of different reasons. The first being, it gives you complete control of your situation. As a young adult you can't control where you grow up, how tall you are, what you look like, or many other things. A lot of these uncontrollable pieces may cause stress or worry. One thing you can always control, however, is whether you are willing to go to the gym and pick up the weight in front of you. I skipped 1st grade when I was a child and went directly from Kindergarten to 2nd Grade. I was already a naturally small kid, however this decision to move up a grade turned me into the class peanut. I was mentally and physically bullied for several years due to being smaller and younger than everyone else. I struggled a lot with self-confidence and social skills as a child as a result. I once got punked out in the hallways so bad during middle school, I still shake my head thinking about it to this day. I would purposely keep my birthday a secret, because it only became a day where I would get picked on for being so much younger than my classmates. This social life only added fuel to my fire for sports, where I always felt confident around my teammates. I was able to isolate myself in a separate world from school where I was in control of my success, starting in the weight room. My freshman year of high school I was 5'4" and a menacing 115 pounds. I began to fall in love with the weight room once I discovered it gave me the ability to directly change these circumstances. As I developed strength in the weight room, the results translated directly to my self-confidence as well. Doing pushups before bed every night was a habit my father instilled in me at a young age. I started doing ten each night at age eight, eventually progressing all the way up until age thirteen where I would do a set of 75 combined with ab exercises. My father, at the age of 62 still does pushups every single day to keep himself in shape. Like many young athletes, although I was undersized I was always one of the better performers on my team and I was in great shape. During high school, my father began waking my older brother and I up at 5 AM to go work out at the gym or run a mile down the street before school. My father was always ready to go when he woke us up. Once my older brother and I were ready we took off down the driveway at the same time and returned whenever we finished. This became routine and developed a sense of work ethic and enjoyment in the process of working out. This is an important aspect as we continue to discuss the weight room– mindset and attitude. What is your intent as an athlete in the weight room?

My intent in the weight room could be described as obsessive. I fed off any player pushing more weight than I was during a workout. I refused to miss a workout, and even took it to a new level as an underclassman. I almost reached the point of being disciplined at my junior college for using the weight room during inaccessible hours. In simpler words, a few teammates and I regularly trespassed in the school weight room after hours. Marley Allison, DJ Olmstead, Joe Eason, and I jammed a small rock in the door knob that allowed us to have our own private 24-hour access to the weight room. The door would close all the way, but the latch wouldn't shut. There was a small bend in the metal that allowed us to grab the top of the door and pull it open from the outside while it was "locked." We would drive to the school at around 2 AM and open the weight room. It was every athlete's dream: dark outside, low lights and loud music, with an entirely empty college training facility. We had to play hide and go seek with the security guard a few times, as they came in through the doors and we immediately paused the music and began ducking behind the desk and hiding. They walked all throughout the weight room, shining their flashlight before eventually leaving. We got caught twice during daytime hours by our coaches, and after strict warnings not to, we continued like the idiots we were. The third time, our head coach came in giving a tour to a recruit and his parents. They entered right as we had a very provocative Meek Mill song blasting on the speakers, we froze as the parents looked at us in confusion. Our coach told us if we used the weight room without permission one more time, he would kick us off the team. We heard the message. In reflection, I'm not sure how we didn't see a problem with what we were doing. This is an example of being blindly naïve, we had no right to disobey our coaches and use that weight room without permission. None of us had a huge role on the team at the time, but we were hungry to get better. Simple as that. All three of those teammates would go on to play Division I football after transferring. I was the lone Division II product of the group– apparently I was missing something from those workouts.

The second reason I loved the weight room is because it held players accountable, honest, and humble. I can't recall the amount of times players got humbled in the weight room. It is you, gravity, and the weights on the floor. Either you are strong enough to move it or you aren't, it really is simple. There is an attendance sheet with X's and blank spots. The players with the X's are usually the players competing during games and staying healthy. While the players with blank spots act confused when they struggle to earn play time during the season.

The last reason I loved the weight room was the bond it created within a team. The weight room and locker room are typically where a football team's best dancers are noticed. There is something about completing a workout with your teammates next to you that creates a sense of trust and confidence in each other come time to perform. You're much less likely to give up on that set if you have dozens of guys screaming at you.

Quick Advice to Succeed in the Weight Room:

- Follow a plan. Do not walk into the weight room each day and wing it. There are hundreds of proven programs for athletes that are cheap or free. None of them include curling in the mirror for twenty minutes.

- Allow your body time to recover. More is not always better. I learned this the hard way after struggling with injuries. The weight room is about becoming as strong as possible while also actively preventing injury.

- Any successful athletic lifting program places an emphasis on lower-body strength and performance over upper body. Nearly all athletic movements begin from the ground up.

- Take time to focus on therapy and pre-hab. Prevent injuries on the field and in the weight room by not skipping on the warm-up and pre-hab exercises, take them seriously. The warm-up should have you sweating before you work out. After the workout you should be spending a minimum of ten minutes foam rolling, stretching, and cooling down.

- Leaders are the first one in and last one out of the weight room. Being a leader may include picking up others weights they left behind. Take pride in the program and facility.

- Remember the purpose of the weight room: to become a better athlete. You are not in the weight room to get a swimsuit modeling contract. Too many times kids get caught up doing exercises for aesthetic reasons that don't translate to their sport. Focusing on getting a spring-break body will find you wondering why you're finishing last in sprints.

- It's possible to make a name for yourself as a successful athlete on the field, without pushing yourself in the weight room; however, there are no successful athletes that make a name for themselves in the weight room. Elite athletes utilize both to become better.

There are predominantly two perspectives that athletes have toward the weight room in my experience. It was either an A: Requirement or B: Opportunity. You should take a long hard look in the mirror and evaluate your goals if you see the weight room as a requirement. These athletes will typically end up injured or buried on the depth chart once their natural talent catches up to their lack of work ethic. Whether that be at high school, collegiate, or even professional level, it will eventually catch up. Every time you step into the weight room it is an opportunity to become a better athlete. I could not bench 135 pounds my freshman year of high school, yet by my senior year I was benching 275 pounds. While you are going through puberty and your body is pumping out hormones, it is important to capitalize on the benefits of weight lifting. The weight room is a critical piece of any athlete's journey. I am not contradicting what I said earlier: you should be on the field more than you are in the weight room. However, they are still equally important when it comes to succeeding and thriving in high school and collegiate football. You can expect when you get to college to have 6 AM lifting sessions all summer long, as well as during the season depending on if you are a travel, non-travel, or redshirt player. You will have a specific program to follow, and phase testing to measure your progress. Many colleges even take photos to use as visual progress measurement. My progress photos happened to put my ridiculous tan lines on full display. The single most important piece to the weight room for any athlete is consistency. It doesn't matter if you go hard the last two months of summer if you were slacking off partying, playing video games, and eating junk food the rest of the year. The best athletes were in the weight room the day after their last game of the season. Consistency in effort, consistency in attendance, and consistency in attitude. We will now dive into how you can best use your time as an athlete to develop, and what to expect from weight training at the collegiate level.

While you are in high school, chances are you have a lifting program from your football coach or strength and conditioning coach. However, attendance and measurement are probably not as supervised or tracked as they are at the college level. One of the most common mistake young athletes make is training to *look* good, and not training to *perform* good. Of course, elite athletes often have aesthetic physiques as well, but it is a result of training for strength, speed, and durability while maintaining a balanced diet. There are several exercises young athletes tend to love that really don't translate to the football field at all, such as: bicep curls, calf raises, tricep extensions, quad extensions, and a plethora of ab exercises. Athletes are in environments where you engage with free-weight opponents (another player) rather than a fixed object. Weight room training for athletes should be heavily focused in the usage of free weights, dumbbells, resistance bands, and medicine balls. Machines require less balance, body control, and spatial awareness. Your workout, whether it is an upper-body or lower-body focused day, should nearly always include a heavy compound movement and an explosive plyometric movement. There are numerous studies crediting the benefits of plyometrics training for speed and change of direction. Athletes inherently are required to perform complex, explosive, and high-velocity movements during practice and game situations. It is crucial that your training replicates this inside the weight room.

The main focus needs to be primarily on developing lower-body strength and size as an athlete before college. Most strength coaches will support the fact that the majority of athletes come into college on the opposite end of the spectrum, where their upper body is disproportionately developed. This is a product of the all-too-common mindset discussed earlier of being overly concerned with the look in the mirror and the Combine bench press test. Your legs are who you are as an athlete. One study collecting data from over 5,000 NFL Combine participants tracked their success as NFL players. The research calculated average performance numbers for each position according to their status as either an All-Pro, Pro-Bowl, or No Accolade. The trend shows a more noticeable difference between All-Pro and No-Accolade performers in the events of forty-yard-dash and vertical jump in comparison to bench press. You may be the fastest kid on your team without lifting weights. This may lead you to the conclusion you don't need to squat or lift weights. You are wrong. I am telling you, when you get to college whether you are the fastest player or not, you *will* get injured if you haven't built a foundation in the weight room. Athletics are more physically demanding in college, and something as simple as a pulled hamstring can ruin your season. Following a program that is consistent and science based will be your best bet to seeing measurable gains and staying healthy.

In college, you will ultimately be at the mercy of your head strength and conditioning coach. In the offseason you may be able to do some of your own workouts, however 90% of the year you will be following the program supplied by your coach. In order to be a strength and conditioning coach there are rigorous academic and certification requirements. I highly recommend buying in completely, and trusting the expertise of your coaches, regardless of whatever workouts you do in your free time. I had two vastly different approaches between strength coaches in my two programs, each effective in their own ways. The fact of the matter was, in both programs the guys who worked the hardest always saw the best results regardless of what the workout was. Our strength coach in junior college, Kate Engard, is a phenomenal trainer who currently works for the Phoenix Hotshots of the Alliance Football League. She always approached training with an educated, no-bullshit perspective that produced results. Our team lifted on Sundays after our games in season during junior college. It was not uncommon for players to come in that would have "light" injuries, be hungover, or just simply be unmotivated to workout. In one instance, two of our starting linebackers with multiple Division I offers were acting sluggish and whiney the day after a game. Coach Kate told them to grab their shit and get out of her weight room. She did not accept excuses or half-ass effort. Having been a collegiate athlete, and earning her master's degree in human movement, Kate was an awesome mentor and coach due to her ability to relate to her athletes' circumstances. She put us through a few notorious workouts, such as "Crazy 8's Barbell Workout," endless bleacher conditioning, and a few others. For one memorable summer workout, Coach Kate took us out into the Arizona desert behind campus and had us flip tractor tires in the dirt for a mile each way. Dust was flying everywhere, knuckles were busting open on the ground, and it was close to 100 degrees outside as we cooked in the Arizona sun. She pushed us to be great. Collegiate scouts and coaches would frequently stop by the weight room in junior college to ask Kate how certain players' effort and attendance was. You can bet your coach is going to be honest since you are representing them. So if you aren't in the weight room when you are supposed to be, the recruiting trail may stop for you there. Coach Kate told a story of a coach from a major Division I football program stopping in the weight room looking for a teammate of mine. They asked Coach Kate if he had been in the weight room that day, and she responded no. Turns out the player had told the coaches he was heading to the weight room, so the coaches followed through to check it out. Remember, you are always being evaluated, even when you might think no one is paying attention.

The culture of our program in the weight room was encouraging for growth. Most of the team didn't need fancy facilities, or any external motivation to get work done. Every player in the program was fighting for a common goal, an opportunity: the opportunity to make it out of junior college and prove everyone wrong. This created a competitive environment in the weight room. Coach Kate always kept morale high and served as an amazing coach during my time at Scottsdale Community College. This may not be the reality for every campus across the country, however. Our junior college hired a new strength and conditioning coach for my final season and the atmosphere in the weight room was completely different. The coach wasn't a bad technical instructor, they just struggled with authority and holding players accountable. The standard for excellence slipped, and it was felt within the program.

Regardless of your coach, program, or teammates, the responsibility ultimately lies on yourself to handle your business and get better every single time you show up for a workout. The days where you don't feel like lifting, or you have a flat-tire, or you missed your alarm and woke up late are the days where it is truly a test of your willpower. Push yourself to fight through the most difficult days and you will find yourself feeling much better after the fact. Heading into my senior season I expected nothing less from myself than perfect attendance. I lived with three guys on the football team and my car was broken down, so we typically all rode together. I woke them up on several occasions to make sure that we all made it. I never missed a single workout in my college career, but I couldn't participate in my last summer workout. I had missed my alarm and woken up to an empty house with about fifteen minutes until the workout started. I couldn't believe it. I threw on my shoes and began running down the street. I lived far enough from campus that I showed up about five minutes late. Once the gate was shut, it was shut. I sat outside the weight room across from the field, staring at my team on the field for an hour at 6 AM. Once the team finished on the field, they walked over to the weight room, where everyone was surprised to see me. Our coach wouldn't allow me to work out, so I just sat in the weight room and watched the rest of the team lift weights. I wanted to set the example that the weight room was important. I could have easily walked home, but that would have been sending the message I was content missing the last workout. To further emphasize the importance of your mindset in the weight room I will share one of my most memorable experiences as an athlete. I witnessed a kid get cut from our team in junior college for showing up late to workouts in a pair of Jordans. Our coach couldn't believe this player showed up late, without a proper pair of lifting shoes. This proved to the coaching staff that he didn't want to make the team as badly as he said he did. One mistake is all it takes for someone else to take your spot at any given moment. Don't forget your sneakers!

We've covered the requirements and expectations to succeed in the weight room as a college football player. All the energy and sacrifices made training will be nearly useless if you don't pay attention to the rest of this chapter. Your diet will be one of the biggest components of your results from working out.

I did a lot of very ridiculous things to try to gain weight while I was playing football. In high school I drank a gallon of whole milk every day for a month. This was known popularly on the internet as the GOMAD Challenge. Somehow, I was able to convince several of my teammates to do the same. I gained approximately twenty pounds of bodyweight during that time and made serious strength gains on all my lifts. However,

I also gained a ton of body fat, had horrible breakouts of acne, dealt with indigestion, and might have been slower in sprinting speed due to the weight gained. I didn't really care at the time, I just saw the number going up on the scale and justified the idiotic diet plan. The first day I was doing the challenge, I remember not understanding how to pace out the drinking of the milk, since I didn't plan on bringing a gallon of milk to school. I had to leave for the bus at around 6:40 AM on school days. That morning I woke up at five and tried to drink a half gallon of milk before I went to the bus stop. I sat at the computer watching training videos, aggressively drinking whole milk for over an hour. It was about the time I got to the bus stop I realized that I had seriously messed up. As the bus pulled up and the doors opened, I casually made eye contact with the bus driver, before turning around and vomiting into a bush. I avoided eye contact and walked down the aisle to my seat, uncomfortable and embarrassed. A few other crazy methods I tried to gain weight included adding insane amounts of olive oil into my protein shakes, which typically sent me directly to the restroom minutes later. Not too mention it made the shakes taste absolutely disgusting. Another favorite included ordering four chicken sandwiches from McDonalds for almost an entire summer. Not only was I blinded by the obsessive "bigger is better" attitude, I was probably taking years off my own life expectancy with the food I was consuming.

As I matured and developed as an athlete, I learned the role and importance of a balanced diet. I dealt with significantly less injuries on the back half of my career as I took better care of my body. Having a limited budget, I also learned how to make several quick, easy, and cheap meals that are practical for any athlete. The change in my diet made all the difference in my success as an athlete.

NUTRITION QUICK TIPS:

- Stay away from most supplements. Fish oil, a daily multivitamin, and whey protein are the only supplements you should absolutely invest in as an athlete. Creatine can be a beneficial supplement depending on your circumstances, if you are disciplined enough to stay hydrated.

- I believe you should always eat a large breakfast to start your day. It is absolutely necessary to fuel your body before and after workouts and practice.

- Prep meals for the week and bring food to class to eat to save time. "Not having time" is not a valid excuse for not fueling your body.

- The majority of your meals should be cooked at home. Eating out is expensive and generally less healthy than having meals prepared at home. You are also getting much more value for your dollar by cooking. If you are in high school or the dorms and limited to the cafeteria, simply start by making yourself a snack before bedtime each night. I used to eat a bowl of cottage cheese with cocoa powder mixed in.

- You should constantly be drinking water, aiming to consume at least one gallon a day. When my girlfriend first started dating me and tried to describe me to people on campus, she claims she said I was the "white kid on the football team who always has a gallon jug of water." Somehow, that usually made the person she was talking to go, "I think I know who you're talking about".

- Practice being a conscious eater, and check nutrition fact labels on everything before you purchase it. Develop a baseline goal for tracking your calorie consumption daily and building habits to hold yourself accountable.

- As a broke and hungry athlete, don't be afraid to eat meals that aren't entirely healthy all the time. The reality is you must consume enough calories to grow and have energy, and most people won't be able to do this on an organic, gluten-free vegan diet. I ate a lot of boxed mac n' cheese in college and it served its purpose. The important piece is to balance your meals and still try to hit your daily requirements for fruits, vegetables, and water.

We continually keep going back to the idea of intent. Great athletes, leaders, business owners, coaches, husbands and wives, all make choices throughout the day with a specific intent. This is no different for the food you put in your body. I worked in the cafeteria as a cook while I was a junior and senior in college. It would absolutely amaze me to see my teammates come in and order a double cheeseburger and fries with a soda day after day. The decision is a matter of discipline. Here are a few guidelines and suggestions for beginner meals for athletes:

Breakfast:

Bagel with peanut butter or cream cheese, eggs, oatmeal, turkey bacon, bananas, juice, almond milk, rice cakes, toast, cereal bars, fruit bars, potatoes, pancakes, greek yogurt.

Breakfast is an important meal as a college athlete. It is critical to fuel your brain and body for workouts and class. It is easy to wake up twenty minutes before school and pour a bowl of sugary cereal. It is not as easy to set your alarm an extra hour early and cook some eggs, bacon, and toast a bagel. There is a notable difference in mindsets between athletes who sacrifice their sleep and time to make that decision. All the items listed are very cheap and nutritional options for athletes to start their day off well. There is no excuse. So many times, athletes complain they struggle to gain weight, and you ask them what they eat for breakfast, yet they can't come up with a solid answer. Or even worse, they tell you they had toaster pastries.

Lunch/Dinner:

Chicken, frozen vegetables, rice, beans, potatoes, pasta, ravioli, quesadillas, fish, shrimp, ground turkey, turkey tenderloin, pita bread, tuna, mac n' cheese, nuts.

Snacks:

Cottage cheese, pretzels, greek yogurt with fruit, rice cakes, bananas, tuna salad, granola bars.

One common complaint I constantly heard during college while explaining dieting to my teammates was, "A lot of that food doesn't taste good." This is no different than saying, "Staying after practice is hard when you're tired." Everyone knows oatmeal isn't the most exciting meal to eat every day, but it is a matter of discipline and intent. Just do it. Half of the battles on the road to success are just doing things that you really don't want to do and embracing it. Find a way to make it meaningful.

Providing expert insight, Coach Kate has shared her seven secrets to help athletes who traditionally struggle growing and packing on weight and muscle. This advice is extremely important for all the athletes who step on the scale and see that number and become disappointed. I have adjusted the material to be easily understood for younger athletes; the full article can be accessed by email.

Secret 1: Get Compound and Complex

Compound exercises are multi-joint exercises that work multiple muscle groups at once. Here are the compound exercises you can do at the gym in order to help you gain weight:

- squats
- deadlifts
- bench press
- military press
- compound row

These are all compound exercises that hit multiple large muscle groups. If you only did these five exercises, you would still set yourself up with a solid foundation to gain strength and mass.

Compound exercises are preferred for large muscle groups rather than isolation exercises like machines because they work multiple muscle groups synergistically. This improves body-control and intersegment coordination. Coordination is necessary for power and speed development.

When you pair a strength exercise like barbell back squat with a similar exercise that is explosive in nature, like a box jump, this is called a complex set. Complex sets allow the athlete to gain strength *and* train the explosive nature of the movement being performed.

- squat + box jump
- deadlift + broad jump
- military press + medicine-ball squat throw
- bench press + medicine-ball throw
- row + medicine-ball floor jams

Secret 2: Big Legz = Big Gainz

Your largest muscles are in your legs. When you train large muscle groups, your body releases more growth hormone than with smaller muscles, and that's great for building muscle everywhere!

When most people start lifting weights, they jump straight to the bicep curls and chest machines.

Well, the second secret is that if you want to release hormones to help you gain mass, the best way to do that is to work large muscle groups – your legs.

Secret 3: Sprints vs. Cardio

When it comes to maximizing your training, you need to reduce the amount of long, low intensity conditioning that you do. Jogging for 20+ minutes, riding a bike for a few miles, or using the elliptical machine for prolonged time at an intensity less than <80% of your max heart rate are all examples of low intensity, steady-state training. This type of training is aerobic in nature and generally not conducive to making gains in muscle volume, strength, or power.

20+ minute jogs will make it harder for you to gain weight, because you're burning more calories. Long slow cardio also inhibits protein synthesis. So not only are you expending more calories, you're also reducing the amount of skeletal muscle you'll gain.

Build up to doing three sets of ten sprints for 20 yards with a minute-long break between sets. To do this, the athlete starts at the goal line and sprints out of a two-point stance, focusing on knee drive, lift, and acceleration through 20 yards. After the athlete passes the 20 yard line they slow down and walk back to the 20 yard line where they will reset and and sprint back to the goal line as they did before. In this way the athlete has approximately fifteen seconds between 20 yard sprints and one minute between sets.

Secret 4: How Much to Eat

The single most important thing that will determine whether or not you will gain weight is the number of calories that you consume.

If you aren't eating enough calories, then nothing else you do matters–especially if you're a hard-gainer.

If you want to gain serious amounts of weight fast, you need to be prepared to eat a lot. You might think you eat a lot right now, but you probably don't. As an experiment, track the number of calories you eat for the next three days.

If you want to gain mass as a hard-gainer, then you need to eat approximately:

- 6 to 8 grams of carbohydrate per kilogram of body mass

- 1.7 to 2.4 grams of protein per kilogram of body mass

- 0.8 to 1.0 gram of fat per kilogram of body mass

How to Calculate This:

Take your body weight and divide it by 2.2. This is your weight in kilograms. Multiply your weight in kilograms with the above references for your total daily macros.

To determine your calories, take your grams of carbohydrate and multiply x 4cal/g, your protein x 4cal/g and fat x 9 cal/g. Add up the calories and that is your total daily intake.

Secret 5: What and When to Eat

In general you should try to follow this simple formula for every meal.

- meat (or protein) + starch + fruit or vegetable

- chicken + rice + broccoli

- beef + potato + salad

- eggs + potato + fruit

- protein shake + oatmeal + fruit

- A protein-carbohydrate supplement post work-out and continued feedings of carbohydrate and protein every two to four hours after the workout over the course of the day for optimal recovery.

- If you have time to make a good meal, it is always better to eat real food when possible.

- A good carbohydrate to protein ratio for post-work-out recovery is on the order of 2:1 to 3:1 carbohy-drate: protein ratio.

Secret 6: Sleep 8

Good stuff happens to you when you're sleeping. That's when your body does most of the critical repair work on your muscles, and replenishes critical hormones like testosterone, which are important for building muscle.

One of the most common mistakes I see athle make is that they focus only on diet and exercise and exercise are important, but they are not all you need in order to gain weight and build muscle.

You don't actually build muscle at the gym. You build muscle *outside* of the gym. Assuming you stress your muscles with heavy compound exercises and complex training, and assuming you are fueling your body with a good diet of enough calories, then during recovery the body will utilize nutrients to adapt to the training, rebuild, and grow.

It's the time you spend recovering that matters most in the process of actual muscle building.

Secret 7: Less is More

Quality over quantity. Most athletes believe that they need to go to the gym more often. They think that the more you go to the gym, the better.

Now, if you're an athlete who never goes to the gym, this is great advice, because you *do* need to go to the gym more. However, that doesn't mean that you should go to the gym as much as possible.

As you know, when you lift weights you're actually tearing down muscle. If you were at the gym everyday just tearing up your muscles and never giving them the opportunity to rebuild, you're not going to gain any muscle. In fact, you'll actually lose muscle and risk injury. That's why there's an optimal amount of time to spend at the gym every week. Ideally, you want to go to the gym enough times to hit all of your major muscle groups no more than one to two times each week. In addition, when you do go to the gym, you don't need to spend more than an hour working out. Quality reps over quantity! Get in, get out, get recovering.

Be sure to get nutrition, sleep, and recovery on point to reduce the risk of overtraining and injury.

7
TIME MANAGEMENT

YOUR SPORTS CAREER will fly by in the blink of an eye. The last thing you want to do is have regrets as you walk across the stage to get your degree. So often we hear athletes talk about how if they would have changed this behavior or not done so much of that, the end result would have been different. So many times, I've had people explain to me that they were a former athlete before they "busted their knee." They then go on to explain how they were the best player on their team before ending the story with yet another crazy, hard-to-believe excuse as to why they didn't play professionally. Don't be that guy. Every minute counts. When you tap that snooze on your alarm someone else is waking up on the first ring. Juggling school, sports, family, relationships, work, and a social life is more than most eighteen-year-olds are able to handle without the proper preparation and support. I found myself waking up at 4 AM during winter conditioning to cook breakfast while my roommates were sleeping. I like to communicate the idea that there can never be a lack of time, but there can always be a lack of willpower. Meaning, any time someone shares with me the excuse that they "don't have time for that," what I hear is, "I don't want to do that right now." If you told me about a goal you have right now in your life, that you feel you don't have enough time to chase, I will explain to you how to make the time. Therefore, it's more appropriate for most people to say, "I don't have the desire to do that right now." I am taking the time to write this book amidst a full-time job, volunteering on the weekends, playing in a flag-football league, and maintaining strong relationships with my partner, friends, and family. That's because this book is important to me, and the information in here can help countless kids succeed during college. I care about the product I am developing, it has value to me, and that is why I find the time to work on it.

Find the reason, and then find the time. I lived about a mile off-campus and often had to walk to school in sub-zero weather during the winter months. One time, while I didn't have a car, our dryer broke while all my clothes were in the washer. That was the day we were leaving for our trip to "Camp Ripley" during fall preseason. I had to put two loads of wet laundry into trash bags and carry them to the school to use the dryer. I had no time, so I acted. Whenever you think you are out of time, you can always take action. I began walking to school right away, struggling to juggle the huge bags of wet clothes. I made it in time to dry my clothes and head to camp. There were many times I so badly wanted to hit that snooze button during college. Many players did so without shame.

We rarely had perfect attendance at winter conditioning or summer workouts. The truth is that it was a pretty good reflection of our team's record during the season. Luckily, the trend shifted positively, and that same team took giant strides over the summer and into the next season after I graduated. I can take pride in knowing I was a part of the culture change at the time with many of my teammates. However, the point is, everyone is given the same amount of time in a day. It is up to you to decide how to effectively schedule your priorities to make the most out of it.

TIME MANAGEMENT QUICK TIPS:

- Be consistent with your schedule. Don't stay up till 1 AM when you normally go to bed at nine just because you don't have to wake up early in the morning. Keeping your body in a rhythm maintains order.

- Write down your weekly schedule in some format. Whether it be your phone notes, a whiteboard in your room, or a notebook. Include important deadlines and dates.

- Your social life needs to simply take a backburner during the season. This means instead of hanging out in the dorms when you are tired after practice, you either take a nap, head to the library and work on schoolwork, or prep cook some meals for the upcoming days.

- Work only as many hours as you are able to while still maintaining excellent academic standing and athletic performance. Don't lose sight of your academic and athletic commitments pursuing an extra hundred dollars on your paycheck. As long as you can afford to live comfortably, you need to keep your priorities in order. Your academic career is a means to a brighter future with a much higher earning potential.

- Don't make the mistake of sacrificing all your sleep constantly to "grind." It is common knowledge you have to get adequate sleep to perform your best. There will be certain nights where sacrifices have to be made, yes. But this should never be the norm. The goal should be to expect eight hours of sleep each day.

- Force yourself to complete tasks by having a daily or weekly to-do list. Break it down between simpler and more complex tasks, order it to encourage yourself to cross off one item before moving on to the next. This will give you a sense of achievement, and continued motivation to finish your daily or weekly list. This is a great strategy to simplify any goal that seems overwhelming.

I had a "Dream Ladder" written on a sheet of paper during high school. I taped the paper above my bed, and each rung on the ladder represented a step I would have to take to reach my goal. For example, the top said, "Earn a Division I or Division II Football Scholarship." Along the way it said, "Achieve a 3.5 GPA," "Earn All-Conference," "Gain 15 pounds," etc. I had that paper on my wall from my senior year of high school until I graduated college. For some reason no one ever took it down after I moved out, and I never realized it was still up until I visited home on holiday break. While I was living at home it was the last visual I saw every night before I went to sleep. This passive reminder helped with time management by keeping my mind focused on my goals each day when I first woke, and when I went to sleep.

In high school and your younger years, your time is essentially managed for you. You just have the choice to meet the requirements (show up to class and practice), or not (skip class/practice, or show up late). There is a bell ringing in between classes telling you exactly how long you have to make it to your classroom. Your weight lifting period is limited (your coach will leave and the weight room will be locked once it is over). You will go home after practice, and you will live with a guardian who will supervise you. Your bus will arrive at approximately the same time every day. You get the point. It is a lot easier to manage your time in high school due to the support, however it is easy to get lazy and develop bad habits. If you are constantly showing up to class two seconds before you are deemed late, you are not striving for excellence. The point of this chapter is to help shift your mindset regarding the principle of time management. Once you modify your perspective toward time from there never being enough of it, to there being too much of it, you will begin to develop habits that make your time spent more effective. Looking into college sports, you can examine how to best manage your time by implementing some practical habits in different areas of your life.

I was nervous, and slightly scared to be late to anything my first few years of college. Late to a job interview, a football meeting, a weightlifting session, it didn't matter. I probably wasted several hours every week leaving my house incredibly early, just to guarantee I was on time. I prepared for the worst-case scenario every day, so that if there was a thirty-car accident I would still make it to where I was headed on time. This habit was developed out of the sense of being uncomfortable as a walk-on during junior college. I was not going to give any of my coaches any reason to cut me or give me any negative feedback. I had seen kids cut for missing meetings. This obsession with leaving early started off slightly stressful, but eventually developed into one of my best character traits. You see it all the time: impatient people in lines, aggressive drivers, people running through the airport. There are always exceptions, yet I would venture to say that most of the time people are in a rush it's because they procrastinated doing something entirely within their own control. If you can master the art of punctuality and time management, your overall wellbeing will benefit from a calmer state of mind. Even now as a first-year employee in my position at work, my boss has commended how punctual I am with meeting deadlines. These habits are a direct result of my experience as a student athlete and the lessons I learned.

Once you develop the habit of preparing in advance for your schedule, you will find yourself saving time you didn't realize you wasted. Here are a few hypothetical questions for you:

You have a job interview in the morning. Do you prepare your outfit the day of the interview, or the night before?

You just finished your laundry and are putting your dry clothes in your hamper. Do you throw everything in the hamper, causing it to wrinkle? Or do you fold your clothes properly, so you can put them away as soon as you get back in your room?

You are making chicken alfredo for dinner. You finished cooking your chicken and are waiting for your noodles to finish boiling. Do you leave the pan for chicken on the stove, or wash it while the noodles are boiling?

These are very minor actions that most people probably don't think about regularly. The biggest component of time management is intent and awareness. You consciously choose to wash the dishes while you're cooking, because it will allow you more time after dinner to watch your favorite TV show. You pick out your outfit the night before your interview so you aren't stressed out scrambling to get ready in the morning. You fold your clothes as you take them out of the hamper so that they don't wrinkle and are quicker to put away. You may be thinking, okay, but what does this have to do with being an athlete or a student? The answer is, everything.

Every team at every level at every school across the country has that one athlete. If you've played a sport in high school or college you know exactly who I'm talking about. That one teammate that walks out onto the field 30 seconds before practice starts the entire season, messing with their equipment as they casually stroll out onto the field. Meanwhile, there is another player opposite the field who is already sweating and warmed up before the team gets a stretch in. I would argue that the physical effects of that warmup are significantly less relevant to the athlete's level of performance than the player's mindset. Preparation starts with the mindset.

My football career began playing Pop-Warner football in Arizona. I started playing at age six and competed every year until I graduated college. As a kid I could hardly sleep on Friday nights. I would wake up Saturday mornings amped up for the games. The first thing I would do in the morning is put on my entire game uniform, including pads and shoulder pads. My dad was one of my coaches for several years, so naturally we would always ride to our games together. I'll never forget how my father would roll down the windows a few miles before we got to the game as he explained to me, "I'm turning the air conditioning off to let your body adjust to the heat." I didn't understand what that meant at the time, but I believed and trusted in whatever my father told me. As I reflected on that moment as an adult, I realized my dad taught me a significant piece of time management in that moment. Preparation. This is vital to making the most out of your 24 hours in a day. Something as simple as rolling a window down could be the first decision in your day. Making the thoughtful decision will set a standard for the rest of the day. Remember, it is easy to sit in an air-conditioned car, that is taking the path of least resistance- instant gratification.

Managing your time in college will not be easy. There is no way around it. I can remember constantly stressing out over research paper deadlines between work, football, and class. I eventually started charting my schedule, organizing, and setting aside specific time to accomplish my checklist of things to do. By the end of senior year, I had mastered how to spend my time effectively and life became simpler. This system held myself accountable, there were no excuses. This meant that if I planned to be in the library and finish my homework, that was what was going to happen. There is a lot more to life than playing football and going to school. Myself, I had to make sure to make time for my family, job, house chores, class, and girlfriend. This meant skipping hanging out with my teammates at times, and sometimes not going to the parties that were tempting. Sometimes I wouldn't have time to attend the school event many others were going to. When it came to my relationships, I happily made time for the people that were my foundation. I never lost sight of what was important, always finding time to connect with friends, girlfriend, and family members. For some individuals this may be logging on to their gaming system to play Fortnite with their high school buddies. Sometimes you will want time to yourself to just forget about your schedule and relax. Take some time to enjoy one of your own hobbies aside from the sport you love. Every player on every team has unique family situations, different interests, and separate schedules. However, everyone has the same requirements and the same amount of time in a day. All the fillers and choices in between are dependent on the intent of the athlete. Let's dissect how to best manage your time between the three major components of your schedule as a student athlete.

Academics:

Show up to class early. Have a planner for your assignments and deadlines. Make sure you set aside time for outside learning opportunities and service projects on campus. I participated in the MLK Jr. Day of Service both years I attended Concordia-St. Paul because it was important to me. It goes back to intent– if something is important you *will* find the time. This meant preparing my schedule weeks in advance to be sure I would have time to volunteer. A key concept of time management in school and academics is prioritizing your classes and workload. If you know you struggle with chemistry, but you excel in writing, it doesn't make sense to put off your chemistry project until the last minute in order to complete a discussion board post in writing. If you are enrolled in four classes, it is unlikely that each class will require the exact same amount of time put in. Identify which classes and subjects you struggle with. Prioritize and emphasize the time you dedicate to these classes. One semester during junior college I dedicated ten times as much time into chemistry as I did in all my other classes combined. I simply struggled with the material and really didn't understand it well until I reviewed it many times over. Once you prioritize your time between classes, the next step is to prioritize it between projects and assignments.

By far the biggest mistake I saw my peers make time and time again during college was waiting until the end of the semester to work on their final papers and projects. It is not uncommon to be assigned eight-to-twelve-page papers in each class as a freshman. This type of volume writing was never required for me or many of my peers in high school academics. So many students will wait until the week of finals, buy a few energy drinks, and pull back-to-back all-nighters to write a mediocre paper and scrape by with a C-. The suggested approach is to write about one page each week. This makes the work less stressful, improves revisions, and puts out a higher-quality final product. It makes the traditionally most stressful time of the semester relatively easy once you have your papers completed. It was a good feeling as a senior knowing my papers were completed as my teammates and friends complained about having to cram them in last minute. I didn't follow this methodology my first few years. In fact, I learned the hard way several times even later during college.

My senior year I was required to do a photo story for my online class and community course. The project required us to pick several different locations in the community and take a group of photos to compare the places. I chose to do my project on the discrepancy between park facilities in the suburbs and inner city. There was one problem, though: I waited until the last week of the semester. During the semester, my car broke, and it went from beautiful fall weather to the frozen tundra that is Minnesota, not exactly ideal weather conditions for the city's parks. I borrowed my girlfriend's car the day before the project was due and drove around the entire day to scrape up low-quality photos. Luckily, I had been working on the paper, but it still turned out to be an overall poor presentation.

There were plenty of times where I underestimated the guidelines for a project or assignment and caught myself scrambling last minute. The important take away is to avoid making this a habit or the norm. You want to be completing projects and assignments ideally several days before they are due. Notice I said completing, not starting. This allows you several chances to proofread and finalize the paper before turning it in. Most colleges have a writing center that will proofread and edit your papers for free. This no longer becomes an option if you are finishing the assignment at 11:59 P.M. on its due date. Set aside time to meet with your professor before or after class if you are really struggling with the material in a specific class. It may be difficult to find the opportunity, but it goes back to priorities. Academics needs to always be high on your list of priorities. Without school, there is no football.

When it comes to taking tests, I can remember a time where I would drive with my notebook on the steering wheel, as I headed to class the day of the exam. This was admittedly a terrible method, and I would not suggest it to anyone. I often got mediocre grades on tests my first few years in college because I never studied. Poor time management. As I matured, I realized by studying a set amount of time each night I would learn the material rather than memorize it, and it would become second nature on the tests. Once I did this, I saved myself time because I wasn't cramming for multiple hours the night before an exam or waking up early the day of the test to try and memorize a chapter of material in a few hours. Break down the material and curriculum into sections. Dedicate a certain amount of time to each section each night. This can be as little as fifteen minutes. If you focus for those fifteen minutes, that's an hour and a half a week. The time adds up. You want to get an *education* while you are at school, not just pass your classes. The more often you revisit the material, the better you can retain it and refer to it later. Read the material, write your notes, and review your notes. It is the same concept as preparing for football season. Each week during fall camp you typically "install" a new defensive scheme. However, if you are so focused on the new install each week, by the end of fall camp you will forget the most basic structure of the scheme. Review! If you follow those couple bits of advice for academics, your experience will be more productive while dealing with less stress.

Athletics:

I was the type of guy who took my personal preparation to borderline stupid levels. Every minute of my day was important to me when it came to football, especially as a younger player. As I grew older, I took it to less extremes, but still maintained good habits. I usually woke up a few hours before wake-up calls on all road games to go down to the hotel lobby and watch film. I don't like sleeping in. I was always early to the practice field, and often times the last one off. I worked out almost every Monday (our off day) throughout my college career. I used to hit the field between classes at junior college, going to lectures afterword dirty and sweaty. I knew I would have time later in the afternoon to shower. I don't say these things to try and sound as if I was always doing more than everyone else and I was the perfect athlete. That couldn't be further from the truth. In reality, there were always several other players doing the same exact thing. But between myself and those others, it was still less than a quarter of the team. As you get to higher levels and more successful programs, players practice better preparation in the skill of time management. In National Championship caliber programs there are going to be a higher percentage of players showing up to the practice field and weight room early. There are a few ways as a student athlete you can best use your time for your sport.

Avoid scheduling night classes. The evening is time to watch film, recover, and mentally reflect on your day. The transition from football to class is a difficult one mentally and socially, never mind having to physically undress and take off all your pads directly after practice then walk across campus. Several teammates during my career prioritized showering and changing after practice, only to show up to class late. This is a horrible use of time and was typically a result of scheduling those night classes. Secondly, always show up to practice and meetings early. Review the previous days' installment, go over your notes, and study your film. With the current technology, there is no excuse to not do this. You can show up to meetings fifteen minutes early and pull out your phone to watch film. I typically wore my practice pants with pads inserted in them to meetings. My coaches and teammates usually laughed at the idea, but it saved me from being rushed after meetings. Inevitably, when our coach would end the meeting with, "We're on the field in five minutes," I could stroll downstairs, grab my cleats, and walk onto the field. Meanwhile, there were guys running across the locker room looking for a piece of practice clothing that fell off their laundry loop the day before.

The biggest tip to managing your time wisely may not come across as a time management tip at all. Don't take it for granted. Every time you lace up your cleats, every meeting you sit through, every time your coach yells at you, and every time you are fortunate enough to suit up for a game. You are in that moment living the reality that many dream of and will never be able to experience. The mindset of going through the motions and surviving each practice will have your time disappearing before your eyes. These are the mistakes that lead to seniors leaving with the, "I wish I would have done this or done that," exit speeches. You want to be the guy who sleeps peacefully when walking away from the game, knowing you gave it everything you had throughout your career. That begins with acknowledging that every time you play the game it very well could be the last time.

People often ask, "Is it difficult not playing anymore? Do you miss it?" While of course I miss playing football, my transition after playing was an easy one. I did everything I could to prepare myself to secure a successful career I cared about. I was able to leave the game I had dedicated sixteen years of my life to, with no regrets. I can truthfully say, I could not have invested any more physical or mental energy into the game than I already did. At times, it certainly didn't feel like it while I was going through it. Once the journey came to an end, the feeling of personal achievement was indescribable. This was because I appreciated every second I got to play the game, and it contributed to the experience of being a student athlete. You will always hear people talking about how they "wish they pursued college football" or "wish they tried harder." If you can effectively manage your time as an athlete, you won't be one of those people with regrets.

Relationships:

I know what you're thinking. This section does not strictly pertain to romantic relationships. Friendships, coaches, romantic partners, members of campus, and coworkers are all relationships that you will have to maintain as a student athlete. This will be an umbrella that briefly discusses each avenue of creating successful strong relationships by finding and dedicating the necessary time to do so.

Looking at romantic relationships and partners, there will be a ton of adversity in any serious relationship during a collegiate athlete's career. Whether it is your high school partner you are continuing with, or a new-found relationship on campus, it will have its ups and downs. The schedule requirements of an athlete quite simply restrict the amount of time you can dedicate to your significant other. This does not mean you cannot have a successful relationship while being an athlete. I am not a fan of the criticisms that "A boyfriend or girlfriend can only hurt your athletic career." This is a blanket statement that simply doesn't ring true in all cases. It is no different than any other stereotype statement, and it holds no merit. A relationship can be viewed exactly as a friendship– the other person is either adding or subtracting value from your life. Finding a partner that legitimately supports and admires your athletic career is the first step. Avoid partners that try to find ways to distract you from your passion or make it about themselves. Toxic relationships can be one of the biggest distractions during an athlete's career. Nearly 20% of college students report having dealt with a verbal threat in their relationship in the last year. On a typical football team this would equate to twenty players at any given time. It is imperative for any college student to recognize the signs of unhealthy relationships and remove yourself from them.

My girlfriend messaged me on Instagram while I was a redshirt freshman, and over four years later, we're still going strong. Our relationship has certainly had its ups and downs as any other. There were times where my obligations as an athlete simply caused me to fail our relationship by not giving her the attention she deserved. Fortunately, we were able to always communicate effectively and work through our issues in the long run. My girlfriend only ever affected my roles as an athlete and as a student in a positive light. Never once did she try to convince me to miss a lifting session, or skip a class to spend time with her. This pressure can't all be placed on the shoulders of your partner, however. This is where time management comes into play; you must find the time to still take your significant other out and spend quality time with them. This appreciation is the least they deserve for dealing with the time constraints of practice, school, weights, and traveling overnight during the season. Be transparent with your significant other about your schedule. If you normally have position meetings after practice every night but your coach cancels them for the upcoming Thursday, let your significant other know so you are on the same page. Remind them on Monday if you are traveling for your game. Remind them what time your flight or bus leaves. These details may seem so miniscule and unimportant that they don't even sound like reasonable advice. I can assure you your partner will appreciate the transparency and open communication. It is about you finding the seconds out of your day to send a text or write a note about what is going on. If you aren't willing to do that, you truly are taking advantage of someone who is already going the extra mile. Spend extra time in the offseason to plan a couple of day trips or fun events to enjoy downtime with your partner. This is an important part of maintaining a strong relationship year-round after the craziness of the season comes to an end.

This is a classic story that represents the craziness that is my relationship. My girlfriend visited Minnesota for my second home game at Concordia-St. Paul my junior season. This was after not having seen each other for a few months for the first time in our relationship.

We had not discussed her moving to Minneapolis recently, and were on rough terms considering the circumstances of distance. She showed up with a huge luggage bag for the weekend trip and I was immediately stunned at the size of it. I remember asking her, "Why is your luggage so big?" and She replied, "I wasn't sure what the weather would be like." I thought nothing of it at the time. Women can be sneaky, fellas. At the end of the weekend she mentioned to me that she had shipped her car to Minneapolis from Arizona and she was moving up to Minnesota to live with me. I was speechless. Mind you, we had lived together previously in Arizona. This was bold even for my crazy girlfriend's standards. This is a story I rarely tell people, but reflecting on it years later, that was one of the ultimate, selfless acts of love. My girlfriend got up and moved her comfortable life of 22 years to join me in a completely new environment to her. If that's not sexy and supportive, I have no idea what is. The lesson learned is, maintaining and thriving in a relationship is all about the want to. A relationship is something you will either find time to make accommodations for or write off as being too difficult and choose to be single. Don't be miserable in a relationship, regardless if it is across the country or across the dorms. One thing should be crystal clear for any athlete in a relationship: if your partner is not entirely supportive of your lifestyle, they either aren't the one for you, or it isn't the right time. If at any point your significant other tries to pull you from your sport, they are discrediting the years of preparation and sacrifices that led to your opportunity as an athlete. One of the most difficult decisions you must make entering adulthood is identifying whether that other person is worth the effort. There is no right or wrong answer collectively as to whether student athletes should be in a relationship or not. One thing is certain, though, it is a waste of time for everyone involved to string along a partner and offer them less than complete effort. That's not fair and it's not right. If it is simply too much for you to be in a relationship at this stage in your life, don't be afraid to move forward. Because eventually that lack of effort will turn into resentment, which will turn into arguments and stress, which will turn into negativity that will ultimately affect your academics and athletics for the worse.

As you go through college, building new friendships and bonds with your teammates, it is important to always remember where you came from. Find the time to connect with your past teammates and friends back home. Stay involved and invested in their personal lives no matter how tight your schedule is. If you are fortunate to be close to home, it should be an easier adjustment. Distance naturally drives people apart, and it can be difficult to maintain ties. At the same time, you most likely won't want to start an entirely new life. Texting, phone calls, Facetime, whatever it may be. Find the time to keep contact with those who are most important to you. Tough times fall on everyone, and close friends and family will always be there to support. I keep in touch with several friends in Arizona, some of whom I haven't seen in several years. It provides me comfort knowing that we are still in touch and care about one another. Sometimes, it is even a simple text message letting someone know that you miss them. This may sound like corny advice, but it is a mature step in keeping strong healthy relationships. Your schedule will never be too busy for you to find the time to reach out. I made time to call my parents weekly at a minimum. Without their support and love I would not have been provided the opportunities that made me so busy in the first place. There should be balance between the new relationships forming and ones that are tested through years.

Lastly, find the time to develop strong relationships with your coaches. Your relationships with coaches can be one of the most critical components of your experience as a student athlete. I have found this to be the most common reason many athletes end up transferring schools. Your coach ultimately controls your life as a student-athlete. Find the time to do what needs to be done to manage this relationship in a healthy manner.

8
TEAM CULTURE AND LEADERSHIP

TEAM CULTURE. WHAT is it? What creates a strong culture? These are some questions we will answer in this chapter. College football may not be exactly the brotherhood one imagines. As I share my experiences and those of others, it is not my intention to speak ill toward any of my former coaches or teammates. The objective of sharing these stories is to serve as a learning point for any athlete reading this. I had the opportunity to play in two separate programs, and deal with turnover between coaches and teammates, as will most college athletes. On average, at least twenty FBS football coaches will change jobs every year, usually losing their support staff with them. My experience led me to play for two head coaches, three defensive coordinators, and four position coaches. The coach that recruited me out of junior college was gone after my first semester after transferring. This is the reality of college football; whether it is a lack of production or a better opportunity, coaches and players are always coming and going. Heading into college, the expectation is that your team will be your second family—one hundred guys that are supportive and will have your back throughout any and all possible problems you will face. This may or may not be the case for you, but there are certainly things you can control to create a positive team culture, become a leader, and build meaningful relationships in your program.

TEAM CULTURE AND LEADERSHIP

- Do not practice passive-aggressiveness with your teammates or coaches. Confront any issues or bad blood early. This allows you the chance to clear the air and move on from the situation productively. Holding grudges, or trashing someone behind their back can only produce a negative reaction.

- Nearly all of your coaches and teammates will be from different backgrounds than yourself. This is one of the most beautiful aspects of collegiate sports. Locker rooms are melting pots of several different racial, religious, socioeconomic, geographic, and academic backgrounds. Use this as an opportunity to learn from your teammates. Open up to them about your own personal life and experiences.

- Initiate conversations with your teammates. The locker room will create relationships that truly last forever; lean on your teammates as a safe place to discuss the struggles you will undoubtedly come across. Your teammates are the ones who can relate to your new lifestyle, not your parents, professors, or friends back home.

- Do not tolerate disrespect from coaches. This is a touchy subject, because every player has different opinions on what disrespect is. Coaching you hard after a mistake is not disrespectful, and yelling at you for missing a tackle is not disrespectful. Disrespect from a coach is a personal attack, or belittling you as an athlete. For example, making you feel stupid or disgraced in front of your teammates for asking a legitimate question. If a coach or teammate is disrespecting you, don't react off your initial emotion. Handle the situation with maturity and discuss it with them one on one. Know your personal worth as an individual and stand up for yourself.

- You will not get along with every coach and or teammate. This is perfectly fine, and a realistic expectation for life, sports aside. The issue arises when your dislike for another teammate or coach affects the effort you give them during the week. When inner turmoil starts to affect performance, this is known as a team cancer or having a divided locker room. Avoid becoming a team cancer at all costs. You don't have to like everyone, but you do have to be everyone's teammate. Any leader is always a great teammate first.

- As a transfer or incoming freshman, the responsibility is on you to branch out and make relationships. You will be seen as competition before you are accepted immediately on the team. Go out of your way to connect with all players and coaches on the team.

- Learn every kid on your team's name and where they are from at the bare minimum. I don't care if you need to study the roster. I cringed when players didn't know each other's names. This is a clear sign you are not invested in your team, and that you are only focused on yourself and your personal goals.

- Leaders do more without being asked, and are always the first to be asked to do something. If you want to be a leader, you need to be willing to take the initiative and do more, while also answering the call from coaches and teammates at all times. You will be the first one to be reached out to for fundraising, community service, and simple favors.

- A great leader can't just lead by example, it's simply not enough. A leader must hold others accountable, coach others, and speak up in times of controversy.

During my freshman season I witnessed my first and only fist fight between teammates during a game in the locker room. We were playing a nationally ranked opponent and were down at the half. Per routine we walked down the sidewalk off the field into our weight room as a defensive unit to meet. It was typically a few minutes before the coaches joined us, and in that particular game tempers were high because we did not play well in the first half. There was a slick-talking running back on our team who was injured at the time, and he was leaning up against a weight rack on crutches. This dude was always making funny comments; I don't think I ever saw him be serious under any circumstances. It was pretty quiet in the weight room and he said something that one of our defensive linemen didn't like. This lineman was a pretty outspoken dude. Within minutes of meeting him you would undoubtedly be informed that he was proudly from Baltimore, Maryland. In fact, it is more than likely you would hear this more than once from him during that conversation. He had no problem confronting the running back's comments, and before you could blink, a padded defensive lineman and running back on crutches were throwing punches in between the weight rack. Half the team didn't even flinch, but eventually a few players rose to their feet to break it up. During the fight there was only one person in the weight room not on the team, an older gentleman who happened to previously be the head coach at our school. He typically would be on the sideline in support. As our head coach entered the locker room, the older gentleman began yelling at him, saying the defensive lineman needed to be arrested. Our head coach was confused, but he didn't even acknowledge the comment. We never discussed the moment as a team, moving forward to game planning for the second half. The defensive lineman started the second half and the running back was still cheering on the sideline. We would go on to finish a comeback victory that game. This was one of several fights between teammates during my career, and every fight taught a valuable lesson about team culture. If two teammates fight, or get into an argument, the issue is usually resolved and everyone moves forward. When teammates thrive off drama, talk about each other behind their backs, and refuse to resolve issues it creates a divided locker room and poor team culture. I am not suggesting that problems be solved through fist fights in the locker room, but it is best to address issues when they arise. I played with a transfer from the University of Texas who claimed they used to blast the song "Knuck if you Buck" and fight with gloves on inside the Texas locker room. I have also heard similar stories from former players at other universities across the country.

The worst passive effect of a negative team culture is when players let their dislike for a coach or teammate affect their individual performance. Every athlete will encounter a teammate during their career they do not get along with. Same goes for coaches, where a player won't respond well to their personality and coaching style. I once had a teammate call me a bitch and tell me that he was going to fight me because our coach told me to substitute in for him during practice. In moments like those, you need to remind yourself that you have control over your own destiny, and college football is ultimately a business model. Also, you should never argue with an idiot. One of the biggest mistakes I made on the back half of my career was letting the negative comments from my coaches or teammates dictate my reality. Every film session on Sunday was the same story, nitpicking and micro criticisms of every detail of my game. I fully support being coached and critiqued, but there is a huge difference between being coached and being criticized. A few coaches and players during my career tended to find something negative within nearly every situation, without ever highlighting a positive. This creates an environment for athletes where it becomes difficult to play with confidence for fear of making a mistake.

A period in my life I'll never forget was my beginning struggles during my junior year after I had transferred. The transition did not go as well as I had initially imagined. As a junior college transfer, the expectation is to earn a starting role immediately and nothing less. I had expected to be experiencing the lavish and flashy lifestyle at a university, as does every high school and junior college player coming in to a new program. I was looking forward to making many new friends and becoming part of a new family. This was not the case for me early on. Having been away from football for nearly half a year, I was underperforming on the field and failing to adjust to my new program. I was buried on the depth chart during fall camp struggling to find opportunities. It was difficult to put myself out there within the team as most older players already had their friend groups, and I was several years older than the freshman. This was also the first time I had moved out of state and been away from my family. Regardless, I tried to carry a positive mindset and remind myself this was not the first time I had been in this situation as an athlete.

A few games had passed to start the season and I wasn't playing much, primarily special teams and the occasional snap on defense. I got my first Division II start on homecoming due to the previous starting cornerback suffering a hamstring injury. In that game, I came up with my first collegiate interception, an unforgettable memory. The Wayne St. Wildcats were driving into our redzone to extend their lead. The quarterback dropped back and rolled out to his left, under pressure from a linebacker blitz. He tried to throw the deep-out route across his body, but I broke on the ball and laid out to make the diving interception. It goes without saying, I was fired up. I without question over did the celebration, running nearly 40 yards after the whistle and high stepping across the field while displaying the ever so popular "let's eat!" hand gesture. It was pure passion on display; this was not a pre-emptive celebration dance, and fortunately for me there was no unsportsmanlike conduct penalty. This brought genuine excitement and energy to our defense and sideline, as it was a huge play in the game. There was not much excitement the rest of the game. We ended up losing the game handily, and there were very few bright spots for our defense in the showing. The next day during film the first comment out of the defensive coordinator's mouth after we watched the interception was criticism of my celebration. Telling me to "act like I've been there before." I guess he never thought to stop and realize I *hadn't* been there before, being that was my first college interception. This comment could have certainly been made on the side or in a personal conversation, yet the coach felt it was proper to criticize one of the few defensive bright spots of the game in front of a group of players— embarrassing me in the process.

Now I realize, a lot of athletes reading this will respond with, "So what? Quit being soft." The fact of the matter is, many athletes struggle with self-confidence just as much as the rest of the college student population. I was no exception. Add this to the fact that most athletes on a team aren't the starter, aren't the star player, and may have not achieved the level of success they are reaching for. These comments can build up and over time create a realm of negativity in the athlete's psyche and confidence. I stand firmly behind the belief that the most successful football coaches can motivate, coach, and critique their players without ever having to damage their players' confidence or self-esteem. In fact, these successful coaches find mistakes as an opportunity to grow an athlete's skill set, not tear them down. Coaches speaking ill toward their players create a negative team culture. There were times during the season where my teammates would ask me why our coach was so hard on me. I usually laughed it off or tried to ignore it, but after it became routine, players were consistently bad-mouthing the coaches in the locker room. It created an "Us versus Them" mentality between certain groups of players and the coaches. This is never a great spot for a team to be in. If you feel a coach has it out for you, it is important to sit down with them and discuss the issue. Many times, coaches can forget what it is like to be an eighteen-year-old kid far from home. It is your responsibility as an athlete to initiate this conversation. College coaches have many responsibilities and it is not possible for them to schedule a meeting every week to check in with their players.

I reached my peak mentally as an athlete during my junior college career. I may have developed physically, and spent more time playing on the field as an upperclassman, but the crucial mistake I made was allowing my coaches to get in my head. I truly lost the crucial confidence I had once played with. As a senior, I struggled every single Saturday to justify my position on the field, when I had every single physical and mental tool needed to perform at a high level in that conference. I had proven that several times during practice and in games. During junior college, the team and coaching staff created a culture of competition. There was no discrepancy in how the players were treated by coaches, and the coaches rarely tried to embarrass us as players. It is important to never allow a coach's comments to influence your mindset too strongly, whether positive or negative. There are scenarios on the opposite spectrum where a player is constantly being praised by the coaching staff and they eventually lose their competitive edge. This can allow players to ease off on the gas pedal and become comfortable. Take positive and negative comments from your coach at face value. When a coach is correcting your technique, take it to heart and apply the knowledge appropriately. However, when a coach tells you that you would have made that play if you were taller, the comment should go in one ear and out the other. The intention of this advice is not to paint coaches as bullies, but to shed light on the reality of my own and several other's experiences. I made the mistake of buying into negative comments and letting it affect my attitude. Don't make the same mistakes I did. There became a point in my career where just based on comments from my coaches I really doubted if I was where I was supposed to be. No matter how strong your bond is with your teammates, team culture can suffer, and personal frustration will develop if those feelings aren't reciprocated with the coaching staff.

My senior year late in the season we were facing a ranked opponent at home. I had finally begun getting into a groove and was beginning to feel and play with confidence once again. One particular moment late in the season nearly caused me to reach a breaking point. We were at a close point in the game and I had been playing one of my best games of the season. Sioux Falls was driving into the red zone and we needed a stop on defense. We were playing man coverage on defense, and my receiver ran a shallow drag immediately off the snap. I had studied enough film and recognized the play immediately, sticking my foot in the ground and driving on the ball. I delivered a huge hit on the 6'4" receiver, jarring the ball loose and forcing an incompletion. It was an exciting play, the defense was juiced, the sideline was juiced, and I let out a war cry as we head to the sideline. I was feeling great. As soon as our defense rallied to the bench, the defensive coordinator came over and said to our group, "Finally Cap makes a play! We have been waiting for that all year!" and then began drawing on the board. I made eye contact with a few of my teammates, who just shook their heads. How were we supposed to play our heart out for a coach who was so comfortable trying to publicly embarrass his own players? This was a separate defensive coordinator from the previous story. These coaches had focused more on their defensive schemes; rather than creating a championship team culture. Learn from these experiences as I write about them and try to form as strong a bond as possible with your coaches to build mutual respect. I was in a situation where I did not have as much time to build relationships with my coaches due to turnover. This created a difficult environment to build a strong team culture as a leader on the team. It will be extremely difficult to become a leader on any team if you do not first have the respect of the coaching staff.

As a player, you must go out of your way to develop relationships with your coaches. I am guilty of not doing a great job of this during my career and the previous stories may reflect some of the poor relationships I had. In junior college, our defensive back group was always hanging around the coach's office and bullshitting in the back of defensive meetings. We were tight-knit— our coach would invite us over to his home to hangout and watch football with his family. At university, we would regularly go bowling during the offseason with the defensive back group and our coaches. These were some of the things that contributed to success on the field more than one would think. We were comfortable with each other, and it was due to everyone branching out and trying to get to know each other. When you have a break during the day, do not be afraid to go sit in your position coach's office and have conversations that have nothing to do with football. Get to know your coaches and teammates on a more personal level, it will directly translate into more mutual effort on the field.

A critical piece of advice related to building relationships with your coaches is: Don't rely on social media or phone conversations. I have personally heard from a few coaches about some of the texts they have received from players that could be described as nightmares. I have had former teammates who would text our coach hours after a game asking why they didn't play. In one instance, we had a member kicked off the team for tweeting his frustration about lack of playing time after a game. In today's age, much of the recruiting process is done via direct message or texting, however once you are on campus you should have as much face time as possible with your coaches. Never address an issue or complaint over text; this is a sign of poor communication skills and can lead to tension between yourself and the coach. Not only does it create a bad image, it is an electronic receipt of your comments, so you better be sure you know exactly what you are saying before you click send. I am a believer in going straight to your coach's door and knocking. Any respectable coach will find time to speak to their players. That is one of the biggest functions of their job, and quite frankly what most of them signed up for. They want to build relationships just as much as the players do—they just have several other responsibilities that are priorities, and rightfully so. At the end of the day, as you go through high school and college you are building skills that translate to employment and professional development after graduation. A critical skill that is being lost in the technological age amongst millennials is the ability to have a difficult conversation and communicate effectively. Whether you are unsatisfied with your playing time, or struggling financially and looking for a scholarship improvement, these conversations are only appropriate to be had in person. To expect any reasonable outcome or favors from your coaches in these situations, you better have done a good job of building a relationship with them prior. You will never be able to control the scheme your coaches run, or how they structure practice, but you can affect how strong your relationship is by investing time into it.

When it comes to the X's and O's, there may come a point where you disagree with your coaches. Do not get in a power struggle; as an athlete you must respect your coach's knowledge. When you argue with a coach over their coaching points, not only are you putting yourself in the doghouse, you are putting yourself above the team. If you don't want to place your right foot in front of your left foot, you are telling your coach and your teammates that you are going to do your own thing. This usually leads to doing your own thing on the sideline, and eventually doing your own thing on the weekends because no one wants to be around the player who is solely focused on their own wants and needs. There were plenty of times I disagreed with a coach's technique. I thought my way was the best way simply because it was what I was most comfortable with. After arguments, and getting yelled at, I realized I needed to use the technique that my coach was teaching. If nothing else, a coach isn't likely to play an athlete who doesn't believe in their coaching. I will confidently make the statement that I had some of the best footwork for a defensive back at my junior college and university. This does not mean I was the best defensive back, but my footwork was always on point. All my teammates quickly discovered I was terrible at catching, basketball, freestyling, dancing, and many other things, but no one ever told me my footwork needed improvement. Anyways, I was recruited to play safety at Concordia-St. Paul signing my letter of intent with that in mind. Once I arrived, I was told I would be playing cornerback by my coach after we finished stretching on the first day of fall camp. I also learned we played from a half-turn technique, which was completely foreign to my skill set as a football player. I was extremely frustrated, since I felt like I was starting over. Once I became comfortable, it proved a vastly superior technique to play the defensive scheme we ran. I still use that technique to this day while playing in flag football leagues, and it feels like second nature. If I had never resisted the change initially and viewed it as an opportunity to become a better player, I may have found myself on the field quicker after transferring. I was labelled by my coach as having a "JUCO Mindset," which carries a negative stigma in most coach's offices and translates to being selfish and unwilling to be coached. While I didn't agree with it at the time, in retrospect there were times where I was stubborn in my ways. As you enter college, one of the easiest ways to develop a strong team culture is by fighting for and believing in your coaches, regardless of whether you agree with them or not.

Play calling, game management, practice schedule, none of those are your responsibility to oversee. Whether you hate it or love it is irrelevant. A coach will not change the defense or offense they have been running for twenty years because an eighteen-year-old kid whose only credentials are a playbook they designed on Madden doesn't agree with it. Let the coaches that recruited you or came into your school do their job. I would not have appreciated if my coaches came into the restaurant I was working at and told me I had on the wrong pair of shoes, and that I was holding the drink tray incorrectly. You shouldn't tell your coach their play calling is wrong. This can only impact team culture in a negative way. I did not follow my own advice as early or as effectively as I could have, because I didn't know any better. Arguing with a coach about their scheme will only lead to resentment. These guys have been coaching for as long as their players have been alive most of the time. As much football as you think you know, your coach will always believe they know more than you, and that is justified. Let them do their jobs, and regardless of the play call or practice schedule, and you do yours. This means flying around with intensity and maximum effort one hundred percent of the time. This is how you earn a coaching staff's respect and build strong relationships. This is how teams build a culture of trust and brotherhood. As I continue to discuss team culture and leadership, I would like to highlight a letter of recommendation my head coach from junior college supplied in request for my application to become team captain as a senior.

"To Whom It May Concern:

My name is Doug Madoski and I am the head football coach at Scottsdale Community College (SCC). I was asked by Andrew Capirchio to provide this letter of recommendation on his behalf for your review of his application to be a captain in your program, which I am honored to do.

"Cap," as we affectionately referred to him during his time at SCC, was a tireless worker and leader with a team-first mentality. Andrew came to our program as a walk-on with no guarantee of making the team and managed to make a profound impact on our team's success both defensively and on several special teams. He was a member of back-to-back Valley of the Sun Bowl teams here at SCC, where he worked his way from the bottom up to the point where he had the opportunity to start numerous games for us during his time here.

Cap was never a guy that I had to worry about in regards to working hard and doing things right academically, socially, or athletically. It seemed as if that is the only way that he knows how to do them. He simply does not look for shortcuts, or let a moment define him; rather, he works as hard as he needs in order to get the job done, and he demands the same from those that he surrounds himself with. As a coach, "Cap" is one of those guys that you wish everyone would be like: the first to arrive, never has an excuse, coachable, and willing to always go the extra mile for the betterment of the team.

I often say to coaches that we look for those guys that are available when the kitchen gets hot. To clarify such a statement, I simply mean whom can we depend on regardless of the situation? Too often coaches get caught up in measurable attributes and discount the sheer will and heart of people. Without question I would argue that Andrew is both always willing and always ready to put his best foot forward and be successful. In this industry we as coaches frequently throw around the statement "if they all acted, played, or worked like so and so then we would be so much better." I know during Andrew's time with us I made that statement about him several times. I would highly recommend him as a captain for your program as there is no doubt in my mind that he will both inspire others to be a better version of themselves, and that he can handle all of the responsibilities that come with such an honor.

Should you have any further questions, feel free to reach out directly to me."

The relationship I had built with my coaches was not glamorous. I earned respect and built trust in my coaches by handling my business, and not questioning their motives or intent. I gave my team every ounce of effort I had every day. These relationships translate to successful team culture and a positive atmosphere for student athletes to develop as people. I am forever thankful for the opportunities I had to grow and develop thanks to my coaches and teammates at each of my respective schools. Team culture is a critical part of the student-athlete experience. There will be highs and lows, and more drama than the average person probably expects. Within my years as a student-athlete I witnessed teammates having sex with another player's significant other, fist fights inside locker rooms and off campus, and numerous counts of theft between teammates. I've also witnessed teammates support another teammate experiencing homelessness. I've seen teammates take each other into their family's home for holidays. I've seen teammates rally and visit each other after injuries or hardship. I've seen teammates make an impact in their community and on campus with volunteer efforts. It won't always be pretty, but there is beauty in going through the struggle with your teammates.

"Cap was born with good credit score!" This was one of the favorite lines of one of the defensive backs my freshman year. I also made the mistake of wearing "whitey-tighteys" in the locker room. I was under the impression grown men didn't care what underwear each other wore— boy was I wrong. I was the victim of many roast sessions that year. My teammates respected me because I was laidback and didn't change who I was to fit the mold. Once I transferred, I was known as the kid who wore "Fubus with jean shorts" on my official visit. Apparently, my fashion style wasn't as popular as I thought. This was a part of the game all athletes remember, the bus/plane rides, hotel trips, meetings, etc. I can never forget the "at the family reunion" roast sessions on the bus, or the gang wars between bunkers at Camp Ripley. At Concordia-St. Paul we had the unique opportunity to go to a military base in Northern Minnesota for a week during fall camp. We slept in the barracks on cots and engaged in several team-building exercises the coaches put on for us. What the coaches didn't organize were the rap battles outside at night, or the gang wars between pods. Freshman would return to the bunkers with a bloody lip explaining, "The boys over in pod four got my ass." At the end of our military experience we stopped at a lake resort for a day of relaxation. Who could forget one of our loveable lineman getting phone numbers and winning over the mature ladies at the bar. The experiences you have as an athlete will be moments you cherish forever, but the moments are that much more meaningful when the culture is that of a family. How can you as a player help influence and create this culture?

All the time you spend off the field with your teammates greatly outnumbers the hours on the field. The simplest piece of advice that can help your team culture become a positive one is simple: Don't be an asshole. I had the pleasure of having one of my teammates try to get with my girlfriend over social media. That's being an asshole. This happened while I was a line cook in the school cafeteria. The next day that teammate came in for breakfast, and I confronted him. We had an argument and he eventually apologized. That teammate and I played the same position and had never gotten along particularly well, but after the fact he apologized like a man, and we were able to get along. We never became best friends, but we respected each other enough to not make it a continuing issue. Being a part of a sports team is no different than being a part of a family, a workplace, a church, or a classroom. The same rules of society apply, support each other when it is needed most. There will be plenty of intense competition and emotion on the field; don't be that guy who carries it off the field into the locker room, or even worse carry it with you everywhere you go. I realized through my years of being an athlete that everyone is raised differently and embraces different cultures. With that being said, everyone doesn't have the same understanding of what being an asshole actually means. Here it is in plain English:

- Don't pursue a teammate's significant other. Just don't do it. If they are broken up, how long you wait depends on the size of your campus. I'm kidding. Still don't do it.

- Don't get mad at your teammate for stealing (otherwise known as earning) your playing time. They either outperformed you or outworked you. If you disagree with that, your frustration should be with the coach, not the player. You need to be as excited for any teammate's success as they are.

- Be willing to help your teammates out. I always was giving rides during junior college because I was fortunate enough to have a car. Many of my teammates were thousands of miles away from their families and struggling financially, a simple car ride could go a long way in these situations.

- Football is a team sport, treat it as such. Don't be the guy who posts his highlight of an interception on the ride home after your team lost 54-0. You will quickly lose your teammates' respect if it is obvious you only care about your own success.

If you aspire to be a leader, as I hope everyone reading this does, there are a few extra measures you will have to take to improve your team's culture.

- Hold your teammates accountable. Call people out in the weight room who are skipping reps. Text guys who miss workouts. Don't give your class notes to your teammate who skips class every week. Demand more and expect more out of your team. You must set a high standard yourself to demand this from others. In other words, don't get mad at someone for missing weights if you aren't showing up. During winter conditioning after our 2-9 season, I recognized our team showing some complacency during conditioning. We were always told what the workload would be before the workout— for example three sets of eight sprints at various distances. I noticed a large group of players appearing sluggish and missing their times. Once we finished what was thought to be the last rep, I called for the entire team to do another set. This was long before I was a captain. I could hear some groans, a couple of swear words, and some angry players. It didn't matter, I was trying to prove a point. I was probably the most disliked player on the team in that moment, but I believe players respected it after the fact. The team needs to always be willing to stretch its boundaries. Simple ways to push teammates include doing an ab workout after lifts, staying after practice to work on technique, hosting player led film sessions, or meeting with your teammates to discuss their goals.

- Organize off-the-field team events. Whether it is a house party, a barbeque, or a video game session; it doesn't matter. Find ways to get guys on the team involved and hanging out with each other who may not normally take those steps or leave their dorm room. Not everyone is a partier or a chapel type of teammate, but there are plenty of options for entertainment that everyone can be involved in. A strong chemistry on the field starts with being comfortable with one another off the field.

- Handle disagreements and arguments like a mature adult. Again, this goes back to not posting on social media about teammates, talking behind their back, or going to the coaches right away. The only way to handle issues is by communicating face to face. If you expect your team to be a brotherhood or family, you must treat it like one. This means having the difficult conversations we talked about earlier. Anyone can post a vague Snapchat story about why they are frustrated. This is not a demonstration of leadership and will lose the respect of the players on the team quickly.

• Do more. Simply put, if you want to be a leader the expectations are higher. Community service, academics, practice, weights, and campus life are only pieces of the entire puzzle. The expectation is that you are the first to volunteer and are always willing to drop whatever you are doing for the betterment of the team. I spent time volunteering at our school's call center, coaching youth football, and picking up teammates from the airport after breaks. It was always the same guys volunteering and signing up for these opportunities. These are a few small examples of what you can do to recognize and earn your teammates' respect. One time, my girlfriend and I had returned to Minnesota on separate flights after a trip home. My girlfriend ended up being locked outside of our house in Minnesota and no one was home. I called a few teammates of mine who picked her up at 3AM and made her a bed in their dorm room. That's being a phenomenal teammate and leader. It would have been easy to ignore a phone call at 3 AM.

To conclude this chapter on team culture and leadership I asked one of my good friends and former teammates to share their experience. Steven Hubick is a former walk-on at Phoenix College, who played with me at Scottsdale Community College before transferring to Alfred State College in New York. Steve was voted his team's Defensive MVP and earned 1st Team All-Conference as a senior. Steve recently graduated with his Bachelor's of Science in Nursing. Many athletes may find his story relatable with no recruitment out of high school, and little recruitment out of junior college. His work ethic and perseverance carried him to where he is now. With the unique experience of being at three separate schools, Steve had this to share about his experience as a college football player:

"I never had an interest in playing college football, nor even attending college. My entire life, I always wanted to join the Armed Forces and make a career out of that. Due to certain circumstances, I was unable to join. That's when I found myself as a walk-on at Phoenix College. Formerly attending a high school that didn't push football too much, I was in a state of shock. In high school, we never watched film, weren't properly taught technique, and ultimately we just had to show up. I was bombarded with watching film every day and having the coaches scream because my technique wasn't up to par. I had to bust my ass every chance I got to ensure I obtained a position on the team. About a month into practicing, I was receiving reps with the starters, and was considered the starting outside linebacker. Shortly after, I severely pulled my hamstring. I couldn't walk, couldn't practice, and saw the position that I worked so hard to get disappear before my eyes. The coaches didn't really talk to me anymore, as many coaches live by the "what have you done for me lately?" mindset. Injured and unable to practice, I wasn't providing them any value. I proceeded to redshirt my freshman year, played my sophomore year at Phoenix College, and then transferred to Scottsdale Community College as a redshirt sophomore. This was my first taste of an elite college football program. Every aspect was dominant: The training, the coaching staff, and most importantly, the players were the cream of the crop. Without this school, I wouldn't be half of the player I became in the following years.

For my final two years of college football, I attended Alfred State College as a strong safety. Coming from a junior college, I was prepared for anything that I was going to encounter. I hit the ground running the day I got there. Every chance I got, I led, gave my experiences, and tried to push every teammate of mine. Everything a captain should do, I did. Unfortunately, the head coach didn't think so. I like to compare this coach to a dictator. He needed all the power, he didn't listen to his players or other coaches, and did things for himself rather than the team. He is one of the main reasons that the college had such a struggling football program. Throughout the season, it was me and my teammate Brandon that controlled the defense. Going into my last game, Brandon had 98 tackles, I had 99, and the next closest defensive player had 50. Brandon was a sophomore, my best friend, and we never had the opportunity to walk onto the field together as captains. One of my most vivid memories of my experience at this school was just before my last college football game. I stepped into the head coach's office and said, "I'm not sure if I am going to be a captain tomorrow, but I believe Brandon and I should be captains as we have demonstrated leadership roles throughout the season. If you can't make us both captains, then don't make me a captain." The head coach proceeded to make Brandon and three freshmen captains the last game.

Throughout my college experience, I've encountered many different coaches, coaching styles, and coaching personalities. The best coaches always put the kids first and did whatever they could to ensure that we were successful. The worst coaches I had looked at it as a business and nothing else. There was no hesitation of backstabbing people or doing what's best for them. Great coaches are hard to come by, and as a player, you have to be grateful when you encounter a coach that truly wants you to succeed on the field and off the field."

9
MENTAL HEALTH

THE LEAST-DISCUSSED STRUGGLE amongst high school and collegiate athletes is mental health. The pressure to perform on the field and in the classroom, the financial struggle, relationship issues, family issues, hardship, injuries, and distance from home are just a few of the many reasons an athlete can experience overwhelming mental health issues. The research is not surprising to note that in annual surveys conducted amongst college students, nearly 70% had described feeling "very sad" within the last year. Upwards of 80% report feeling overwhelmed and physically exhausted. This is a result of difficult demands of college students during a time in their life where they are building their identity, preparing for adulthood, and trying to meet the societal expectations of success. As a student-athlete, you can envision your typical student running around the dorms on fire, and pour some gasoline on them.

We've acknowledged that you will undoubtedly face adversity throughout your life. The difficult part becomes when you try to sustain your mental health amongst the adversity and all your other responsibilities as a student athlete. There were several times during my career where circumstances outside of my control impacted my desire to succeed and/or show up to class and practice, in addition to my quality of life and happiness. I had some oddball injuries throughout my playing career that always seemed to occur at the worst moments. The most disappointing thing about those moments is that my mindset could have been completely adjusted in retrospect. I relied on my identity and success as an athlete with a "do or die" mentality. Meaning, the second I got injured and my future as an athlete was in jeopardy, I became hopeless. I lost sight of my other redeeming qualities and characteristics as person. I saw myself as a football player and that was my complete identity. As soon as I couldn't play, my self-confidence and self-worth plummeted. As a student-athlete, it is crucial that you remember a sport is just one slice of the pie that is your life. You have value, importance, and purpose aside from athletics.

As mentioned earlier, during my redshirt sophomore season I had finally found my way on to the playing field as a starter and was performing at a high level where I was confident I was earning a scholarship. This was a moment during my career where it felt like the entire culmination of all my hard work prior was starting to pay off. My dreams were within reach. Our team had secured a Valley of the Sun Bowl berth and we were still practicing at the crack of dawn during an icy December. Our team numbers were down at the end of a long season and by this point it was really a grind. Most of the top players already had Division I offers rolling in, and a lot of the backups and reserve players thought it was too late to gather interest. This was the perfect opportunity for players in-between the two, like me and a few of my teammates. I saw the window of opportunity. One morning about a week before the bowl game, I had begun to feel awfully tired and sick. Not just a regular cough or runny nose, but something I had never experienced or felt before. Eventually my tonsils swelled up in the middle of the night where I was struggling to breathe. I went to the hospital the next day and was diagnosed with tonsillitis. Tonsillitis is a common infection that is easily treatable luckily. I was given some antibiotics and sent on my way. The only issue was that my symptoms didn't let up at all, causing another trip to the doctor. Turns out, I had mononucleosis (mono) as well as tonsillitis. This sidelined me for our bowl game. My very last junior college football game, a moment I had been looking forward to for three years, was taken from me. The three or four coaches attending the game that had shown interest in recruiting me immediately stopped communication after I was sidelined. Not only did this frustrate me and have my mental health in a tough spot, but the medication I was prescribed turned out to give me an allergic reaction where my entire body from the neck down broke out in a sensitive and painful rash. This lasted for over a week, where I had to continue to go to work and class in pain, tired, sick, and disappointed. When I finally begun to feel the effects of the virus wear off after nearly two months, I had lost over twenty pounds. The physical and mental effects of a common virus threw my life for a spin.

This ultimately caused me to get in a slump for a few months— I never saw a professional or sought out a school counselor. I kept my frustration pent up inside, often leading to anger or outbursts within my personal life. I felt like my friends and family members who weren't athletes simply could never grasp the frustration I was dealing with. I made the mistake of splitting athletes from humans, as if they were two different groups. I did begrudgingly open up to my close friends and family about my issues several times when they asked most of them responding with the same thing: "You fought this hard to get to where you are," or "It would be a shame to give up now." The advice was genuine and given with good intentions, but it certainly was never the answer to cure my problems. So, with zero scholarship offers, twenty pounds lost, and not enrolled in school anymore, I began working full time as a painter during the second half of the year. Daily I would wake up at 4 AM and drive to the site, and I would be home after a full work day around two in the afternoon. I lost all motivation to prepare for my football future, and I began to develop habits that were detrimental. I was at the point where I would come home from painting, smoke some marijuana, and sit on the couch the rest of the day. It was comfortable, it was easy. I had no coach or teammates to push me. This became my daily routine for a few months. I had no one holding me to a higher standard. Eventually some coaches responded to some of my month-old

Twitter messages asking if I was still looking for a place to play. It felt like an ex-girlfriend checking in on you when you found someone new. These coaches were reaching out because I was their backup, but it didn't make a difference. This attention was like a lightbulb going off in my brain. It was almost like a drug in its own. Football was the only thing I had cherished in life, and as soon as it was dangling back in front of me, I felt energized again. This is not healthy for anyone, of course. This attention caused me to refocus on my goals once more and get back to training and preparing. It should have never gotten to the point where receiving a message on Twitter changed my entire attitude. Eventually I was awarded the scholarships I had long waited for and committed to Concordia- St. Paul in April. Never again will I place my entire wellbeing and mental health around one piece of my life. Jobs, significant others, sports, and friends are all replaceable. I'm not advocating for developing a psychopathic mindset of numbing your emotion, but you shouldn't let one failure or shortcoming determine your entire state of mind. There will always be new opportunities.

As I prepared to move to Minnesota, I spent the summer training and enjoying time with friends and family. As the end of summer approached, I attended my cousin's wedding and got ready for the drive to Minnesota with my mother. I packed my bed, a table, a dresser, some clothes, and my wall art of the Grand Canyon into the moving truck. As I left the wedding, I said goodbye to my beloved family members and girlfriend. I had spent the last twenty years in Arizona, the state I called home, and I wasn't sure I was prepared to leave it all behind. It didn't matter though, because it was happening, the wheels were turning.

Once I arrived in Minnesota at my home, I was set up to live with four teammates I had never met or spoken to before. I was the first of us to arrive— our house was in rough shape, and empty at that. There was no TV, no computer, and no Wi-Fi for weeks. I slept on the couch in the living room the first few nights before my other roommates arrived. Frantz was my second roommate to show up, and we quickly bonded over our junior college experiences. We spent time doing his patented ab workouts on the living room floor late into the night. We would then wake up early and walk around the neighborhood and explore. Frantz would go on to become one of my closest friends. Although the experience was everything I had prepared for, I would be lying if I said the adjustment wasn't difficult and didn't take a toll on my psychological state of mind. Fast forward a few weeks, and I did not get the starting position I had expected to get, I was working in the school cafeteria several days a week, and I was enrolled in nineteen credits.

Two nights before Thanksgiving my first year in Minnesota I had a severe stomachache while at home. I am one of those dudes who tries to be a tough guy any time I am injured. I collapsed on the bathroom floor as I was about to take a shower and yelled out, since the pain was so excruciating. I called my mother in Arizona and she suggested drinking some milk or going to the emergency room. Classic mom advice.

Well I certainly wasn't going to the emergency room. I told my girlfriend to get me some prune juice, because everyone knows that is how you cure any stomach pain. I laid cradled up on my bedroom floor, sweating and not moving for over an hour before my roommate's girlfriend suggested we go to the emergency room after looking at me. I caved in and got in the car with my girlfriend. Upon arrival I told them I had about an eight out of ten pain in my stomach. This was a mistake. I ended up waiting in the waiting room for about an hour and a half before being seen. Turns out, my appendix had ruptured. The doctor told me he knew for a fact my pain was a ten and that I should be more careful about answering if I came back again. I was scheduled for the next emergency surgery available, the doctor said it was one of the messier appendectomies he had ever seen. I was in the hospital through Thanksgiving and for several more days as I recovered. I lost a ton of weight and missed the first four weeks of our offseason program. I had been injured several times before, but never injured where I was completely unable to exercise. I had stitches in my stomach, and any pressure from working out could cause them to tear.

When you are taken out of your sport for injury as an athlete it negatively impacts your motivation and mood. It becomes easier to skip class or have a messed-up sleeping schedule while you are injured. You may have less desire to leave your house and spend time with your teammates. Injuries will affect everyone differently, but they never produce positive effects initially. Among injuries as a college athlete, I also dealt with getting evicted, relationship struggles, working too many hours, frustration with playing performance, being away from family, family issues back home, losing loved ones, and difficult living situations. What I dealt with was a fraction of adversity in comparison to a lot of my teammates. Young parents, auto-immune diseases, parents and siblings passing away, homelessness, and poverty were some of the more profound circumstances many of my teammates dealt with. A lot of them found ways to persevere and overcome through sheer faith and determination. As cliché as it sounds, football was a saving grace for some of these guys and they will tell you themselves. The unfortunate part became when players lost the game of football, and they let it deter their success. Arrests, ineligibility, and quitting were not uncommon. If some of these players had had the right support system, knowledge, and resources their athletic stories would have undoubtedly turned out very different. Whether you come from a supportive background, or one of independence and struggle, athletics will play a critical role in your mental health. At the end of the day there are endless possibile scenarios that could affect your personal life while distracting you from your obligated duties as a student-athlete. Due to NCAA rules and other reasons, a lot of times coaches can't assist in these difficult situations. Your family may be hundreds or thousands of miles away. The question becomes, what can you do? When you are struggling the most with your mental health, here are some ideas to assist in self-care.

MENTAL HEALTH QUICK TIPS:

- Seek out the school counselor. If you feel you may be clinically depressed or struggling with anxiety the best option is to meet with a professional. Therapy and or medication can be a temporary or permanent solution for many mental health issues. Athletes are proud and expected to have a warrior image and mentality, which can make it difficult for young men and women to open up about their struggles. This thought process needs to be abandoned. Seek the guidance and support you need to be the best version of yourself.

- Rely on your teammates and friends for support. Spending time with your teammates and putting your sport aside can be a great opportunity to take a step back and relax.

- Speak with your professors and openly communicate if you are struggling with a class. Academics can be one of the biggest stressors for a student-athlete. Professors want to see you succeed if you are willing to put in the effort. The simple act of speaking to them after class and letting them know you are struggling can be the comfort you need.

- Let your coaches know. Ultimately, your coaches won't let struggles in your personal life cross over to practice or games. However, they can be a trusted adult to speak to and offer support and guidance.

If a coach knows you are struggling personally, they will still hold you to the same standard, but they may take their foot off the gas pedal when it comes to demanding more from you.

- Find an outlet aside from your sport that you can engage in by yourself to relax. For myself, I enjoyed reading books or watching YouTube videos. It may sound corny, but allowing myself to sit down and watch a few entertaining or educational videos to start or end my day made a big difference in my mood. I needed that peace and alone time to debrief from everything going on around me.

- Keep reminders of your journey. Reflect on your path and how far you have come. This can rejuvenate your thought process and develop that confidence if it is lacking. Every athlete has that moment where they knew they were doing exactly what they were supposed to. Whether it is reflecting on old pictures, memories, or experiences, taking a step back to look at your journey can be a comforting feeling— to realize you have faced adversity before and overcome it. Reminding yourself of your own strength can be the perspective adjustment you need to get back on track to your right self.

A key part of maintaining a healthy state of mind is staying grounded. Often as young adults and athletes in an entirely new environment it can be easy to lose sight of your identity. Make extra effort to maintain close ties with your old friends and family so you can lean on them when the transition inevitably becomes difficult. Remind yourself of your motivation in the first place. Referring to previous tools discussed in earlier chapters, it can be a calming action to write down daily goals and plans to keep your mind occupied and structured. Your own mind will consume your thoughts if you allow yourself to sit in your dorm, skip class, skip rehab, and skip meals in the cafeteria. The snowball effect can quickly let your negative thoughts consume you. This is where discipline is essential. I can't stress enough the importance of being mindful as a student athlete about your own mental health. Often times social media will glorify the life of a college athlete as "the grind" and normalize the struggles and stress athletes carry. This shouldn't be the case. The perspective needs to be changed to normalize athletes stepping away from their sport when necessary to do what is right for themselves. If you ever feel the pressures of college are simply too overwhelming, find some time to take a break and forget about everything, even if it is for 30 minutes. Taking care of yourself is the most important part of the process, because a balanced athlete will produce more in the classroom and on the field in comparison to the overwhelmed athlete. To provide an outside perspective, my former teammate Brian Stuzkowski shared his story of college athletics and mental health with me. Brian was a former walk-on who developed into a starter as a redshirt sophomore, earning a scholarship for his performance. I asked Brian to reflect on his experience as he prepares to graduate this upcoming spring:

"As athletes we tend to walk a very fine line. Although we tend to be our biggest critics, we also give ourselves a lot of self-love in order to maintain a positive mindset. This self-love is important, so that you don't get too down on yourself in hard times. From the outside looking in, we can be labeled as arrogant or entitled. Becoming egotistical is not the desired outcome, but having pride in your accomplishments is a good thing. Proudly own who you are and what you've overcome to get there. The challenges that athletes face daily help create our personal identity. This is very important to remember when faced with injuries, because as athletes, many of us have created a persona based on our sport. Then when we lose our sport, we also lose our identity.

Injuries happen, and they can be devastating. I know this because I myself have faced my fair share of injuries. In the spring of my junior year in high school, I lost my shot at a state run in track for three events due to a partially torn hamstring. I can still remember my mother hugging me while I was devastated by the news. This was my first experience with a serious injury, and it was difficult. Through a strong support system, rehabbing consistently, training hard when possible, and letting my body heal, I recovered from what I thought would be my worst injury in my career. Fast forward to relaunching my recruitment my senior year of high school. I was able to earn a walk-on spot nearly two weeks after signing day at a Division II school. I had realized my dream of being a college football player.

My new mindset was to become a starter. With enough hard work, I did that in two years. My first start in college I was awarded defensive player of the game in a shutout victory. After accomplishing many of my personal goals, I finished in the top ten in the conference for tackles. I felt I was primed for a big season, and everything was in front of me on the horizon. That all changed when, during the winter of my junior year, in an exercise physiology lab, I ruptured my pectoralis major. I was saved from a 315-pound bar crushing my chest only by a set of safety bars set about one inch above me. I remember the tearing sound— what to me sounded like ripping out carpet. I knew immediately I had torn something. I essentially blacked out, and when I came to I was on my back about six feet away from the bench press. Our strength coach was trying to calm me down and assure me everything would be okay. I was taken to a hospital where I was diagnosed with a torn pectoralis muscle and X-rayed for bone damage. The next week I was back home with my family, getting an MRI to evaluate the severity of the tear. The results were returned the next day, and I learned that not only did I have a complete rupture of my pec, but I would be having surgery in four days.

With the anxiety of not only the surgery but having my athletic career in jeopardy, I can truthfully say looking back that this was where I slowly started to dip down into the looming mental illness of depression. On the exterior I would crack jokes and continue trying to be a fun-loving, outgoing person, but inside it was draining. I had my surgery and was put in a restrictive sling for six weeks, and for the first two weeks I stayed at home with my family in my basement. No lights, just watching documentaries by myself, sitting with destructive thoughts of self-doubt. After the two weeks I drove nearly four hours back to school and began doing every available workout without stressing my chest. Exercising was the only thing that calmed me. It was within my control, providing me comfort. I would watch spring practices and critique how I would run our defensive concepts in those situations. In my spare time I would do walking backpedals just to keep my footwork in tune. Once I was able to, I immediately started doing rehab and range-of-motion exercise, as I was told there was the slight possibility I could return before the season started. To me, that was all that mattered. It was all I could think about, but the process did not come without its ups and downs. During the four and a half months I wasn't really a football player, I felt like I had lost my identity and I was no longer me. For the past ten years of my life football was who I was. Just like that, I had lost myself during rehab. Every failed rep or bad day made me think I would never be me again, and the feeling ate away at me. I'm thankful for my family and the friends I surrounded myself with, because if not for them, I might have just given up. Having them to fall back on when I had a nervous pit in my stomach that I couldn't keep going, or that I wouldn't return in time provided me some level of comfort that I wouldn't have been able to afford myself. My support system gave me someone to vent my frustration to. Not just about the injury, but about my life, my sport, and my feelings. I continued to work extremely hard as much as I was able to. I would run and train with the rest of the team in the mornings and then do physical therapy after. After rehabbing for weeks, I could finally reach my hand over my head, which meant I could come do 7-on-7 with the team and participate in football drills. Being on the field with my teammates for the rest of the summer until early August brought some of my identity back. Having not missed a single day of our summer program, I felt confident I was poised to return to form. I was fortunate enough to be cleared two days before fall camp, so I could be a full participant that season.

I came in feeling that I had conquered everything. I began a battle to fight for the starting spot again and thought I was doing well, filling my assignments while knowing the playbook in and out. When I couldn't figure out why I wouldn't get reps with the starters, I approached our coach. The answer I got was that the coaching staff needed to see me make more splashy plays. With a new goal in mind I started attacking every play at practice to try and create turnovers. I kept a count of every turnover and after still not seeing myself move up the depth chart, things did not add up. Feeling sort of defeated, I again asked my coach if I was doing something wrong. Instead of receiving any criticism or justification, I was told, "We know what you can do," and that was essentially the end of the discussion. Somehow, I had gone from a starter to a 4th-string special teams player. I could see how the coaches viewed me in comparison to before, and it felt as if they were trying to move on from one of their older players to try and let a younger one grow. Frustrated, I continued to try my best and hope something would happen.

Game one passed, and due to one of our corners getting injured, my coach told me they were switching my position to cornerback. I welcomed the opportunity as I was so frustrated with my current situation that any chance of playing more was welcomed. Instead, I spent the rest of the season playing special teams and occasionally hopping in for one or two meaningless plays on defense. This would have been enough to deal with, but I also had to deal with pain in my chest and constant belittlement from coaching. There are tough coaches and yellers, but it became a point where I had other players asking me why my coach didn't like me and if I had done something wrong. In one instance I had gotten reamed and shoved on the side of the field by a coach during a game because a referee looked at me while I blocked on kickoff return. There was no penalty, the referee just looked at me. It became a cycle of me wanting to impress them to earn play time, and it backfiring, and my mental health deteriorating. My safe haven and love for the sport of football had become some sort of personal hell that made me uneasy.

No longer could I leave everything aside and lose myself in the game, rather I took the baggage from meetings, practice, and film home with me. I became angry, hateful, and self-hating at that. I would watch practice film and see mistakes by others and wonder why I couldn't get an opportunity. Every little jab and comment would dig in harder, twisting like a corkscrew in a wound that fed into my deeper depression. Inside I was dying, and by week eight I knew I was ready to move on. I informed my coach of my intent to graduate that spring and received the opportunity to walk with my teammates and be acknowledged on senior day. That moment was beyond special to me, and it brought tears to my eyes. Not just because it was my last home game, but because I felt a short-lived peace that I was nearing the end. That day, I didn't play a single down on defense, not even when the game was clearly over. At one point, I even heard someone in the crowd scream to put me in while we were getting torched in the passing game. In that moment I realized that not only did I know I could play, but so did others. For a second time that day, I felt at peace. Every day until the end of the season I would try and create interceptions and force fumbles or big hits just to continue to prove to myself I could compete. Up until my very last day of practice I was doing that.

Once the season was over, a couple of players and some friends convinced me to run track. I agreed, and after my two weeks off I began practicing with the team. I set what was an agreeable goal by both myself and my coaches: to reach nationals. Every day I grew one step closer to what felt like a chance to prove to myself that I belonged. With the open relationship I had with my track and strength coaches, I feel encouraged and capable of accomplishing any of these goals and am much happier trying to attain them. I am not where I want to be, but I am a lot further than I was, and every day I get a little bit closer to my goal.

The moral of my story is that even though athletes get put into a system to perform, we're people too. Athletes feel emotion and that's okay. We get down, and we can suffer just like anyone else. As much as we like to believe that were invincible, we're not. I'd be lying to you if I wrote this and said I am 100% better both physically and mentally, because in both aspects I still have a long way to go. However, after a slight change of scenery and being surrounded by positivity instead of what felt like a coffin that pulled me into darkness, I feel so much better. Your mental health will make or break you. As an athlete you might not think it, but our mind is our greatest asset. It's okay to hurt, to reach out to someone and say you need help— this doesn't make you weak. I wish I would have reached out to some of my friends and family earlier than I did, because I could have been in a much better place mentally, but instead I suffered. Anyone out there that may be struggling with something inside; I encourage you to be the one that reaches out. It's terrifying to admit to someone these truths and make them all the more real, but this is the first step to change. You all can achieve amazing things and can conquer improbable odds, you just need to move forward. To any future or current athlete or coach, remember your words always affect those around you."

CONCLUSION

I WROTE THIS book with a market in mind: my former self. I understand what it takes to succeed in collegiate athletics, and I understand what it feels like to be completely clueless about the process. All the mistakes and experiences in my athletic career turned me into who I am today. For the thousands of young athletes who aspire to play at the next level, I hope you take the advice and stories provided in this book seriously. Whether you find yourself in a difficult situation at a party, struggling with academics, or missing your family back home, the lessons provided can be applied to any situation. I hope you learn what doesn't work well and what does before you get to college, unlike myself any many others. There should be no reason so many student athletes fall through the cracks and fail to finish their degree. *Blessed to Announce* is one resource to help prepare and educate athletes for the reality of the lifestyle they want so badly. It would certainly be impossible to prepare you for everything you will encounter as a student athlete. Life's journey is unique to each individual, and sometimes difficult circumstances beyond your control will come into your story.

My final words of encouragement to you as a reader are: I hope you find the strength and faith to continue pursuing your dreams. Through the highs and lows, those moments will define you forever. Life is short, and you don't get many second opportunities, so make the most of your opportunity as a collegiate athlete. There will come a time where every athlete becomes a former athlete. How do you want your story to finish?

Thank you for taking the time to invest and trust in this book. Feel free to reach out to me at andrew@blessedtoannounce.com or by social media at any time.

ENDNOTES

1 "The First In Their Family." 2016. *NCAA.Org - The Official Site Of The NCAA.* Accessed January 22 2019. http://www.ncaa.org/about/resources/research/first-their-family.

This resource shows the research into first-generation students in the NCAA student-athlete population. This information is relevant to the idea that many freshman student athletes enter college unprepared.

2 *"Graduation Rates."* 2013. NCAA.Org - The Official Site Of The NCAA. *Accessed January 22 2019.* http://www.ncaa.org/about/resources/research/graduation-rates.

The graduation rates for collegiate football players leaves room for improvement. With approximately half of Division II football players not graduating there needs to be an emphasis on college readiness and preparation moving forward.

3 "Understanding Life Outcomes of Former NCAA Student-Athletes." *Gallup Purdue Index-Report,* 2016, 5. Accessed January 22, 2019. https://www.ncaa.org/sites/default/files/2016_Gallup_NCAA_StudentAthlete_Report_20160503.pdf.

Investigating student-athlete outcomes in comparison to non-student athletes can shed light onto the advantages and disadvantages of competing in a collegiate sport.

4 "Understanding Life Outcomes of Former NCAA Student-Athletes." *Gallup Purdue Index-Report,* 2016, 10. Accessed January 22, 2019. https://www.ncaa.org/sites/default/files/2016_Gallup_NCAA_StudentAthlete_Report_20160503.pdf.

5 *"NCAA GOALS Study".* 2013. NCAA.Org - The Official Site Of The NCAA. *Accessed January 22 2019.* http://www.ncaa.org/about/resources/research/ncaa-goals-study.

6 *Huma, Ramogi, and Ellen Staurowsky. "The Price of Poverty in Big Time College Sport."* NCPA National College Players Association, 2011. *Accessed January 22, 2019.* http://assets.usw.org/ncpa/The-Price-of-Poverty-in-Big-Time-College-Sport.pdf.

This data emphasizes the prevalence of poverty amongst collegiate athletes. Many student-athletes are unprepared for the financial struggles not typically associated with college sports.

7 *Hess, Abigail. 2018. "Here's How Much The Average Student Loan Borrower Owes When They Graduate".* CNBC. *Accessed January 22 2019.* https://www.cnbc.com/2018/02/15/heres-how-much-the-averagestudent-loan-borrower-owes-when-they-graduate.html.

Student debt is an epidemic in the United States, it is imperative for students and student athletes to understand student loans and their impact on their financial future.

8 *"The Increasingly Stronger Case For Hiring 'Athlete' Employees".* 2019. Forbes.Com. *Accessed January 22 2019.* https://www.forbes.com/sites/davidkwilliams/2018/09/21/the-increasingly-strongercase-for-hiring-athlete-employees/#750707806785.

The case for hiring former student athletes is strong, evident by their proven track record of discipline and commitment.

9 *Arazi, Hamid, Mahdi Mohammadi, and Abbas Asadi. "Muscular adaptations to depth jump plyometric training: Comparison of sand vs. land surface."* Interventional Medicine and Applied Science 6, *no. 3 (2014): 125-130.*

This data supports the case for athletes implementing sand training into their regimen.

10 Jacobson, Bert H., Eric G. Conchola, Rob G. Glass, and Brennan J. Thompson. "Longitudinal morphological and performance profiles for American, NCAA Division I football players." *The Journal of Strength & Conditioning Research* 27, no. 9 (2013): 2347-2354.

Collected data tells us not all Division I football players are world-class in regard to strength upon reporting their freshman year.

11 Hedlund, David P. "Performance of Future Elite Players at the National Football League Scouting Combine." *The Journal of Strength & Conditioning Research* 32, no. 11 (2018): 3112-3118.

Differences between upper body and lower body strength in relation to sport performance are showcased by NFL Combine results correlated to received accolades.

12 American College Health Association. American College Health Association-National College Health Assessment II: Reference Group Executive Summary Fall 2017. Hanover, MD: American College Health Association; 2018.

College students show tendencies to engage in unhealthy relationship behaviors, this issue can be detrimental to the success of student athletes if followed.

13 *Barnett, Zach. 2018. "FBS Football Has An Equal Or Higher Rate Of Coaching Changes Than Every Other Sport - Except One - Footballscoop".* Footballscoop. *Accessed January 22 2019.* http://footballscoop.com/news/fbs-football-higher-rate-coaching-changes-everysport-except-one/.

FBS football coaches leave or are fired from their jobs at a high rate. It is likely as a collegiate football player your coaching staff will have some turnover during your career.

14 American College Health Association. American College Health Association-National College Health Assessment II: Reference Group Executive Summary Fall 2017. Hanover, MD: American College Health Association; 2018.

College students show extremely high rates of exhaustion and mental wear.